Table of Contents

Introduction

Some studies suggest that the sound of waves lapping against the shore can help soothe a tired mind. Perhaps that's why worries seem to disappear at the beach. If you're reading this booklet, you probably experience something similar when you're creating in the workshop. In this spirit, we've gathered some of the best nautical-themed intarsia projects from our archive, from a lighthouse and pelican to a seahorse and starfish. These projects are perfect for scrollers at every skill level, whether you just picked up a saw or have been scrolling all your life. The booklet opens with a brief section on scroll saw basics, and every project is paired with a materials and tools list, as well as clear instructions, tips, and techniques to build your skills. So, fire up the scroll saw and set sail!

—The *Scroll Saw Woodworking & Crafts* team

Scroll Saw Basics

The projects in this book are achievable with just a few tools, the first of which is a scroll saw. You'll also require a few additional tools, all of which are components of a standard workshop setup: a drill for adding blade-entry holes and different design elements, various sanding machines for finessing the cut shapes, and paintbrushes for applying your finish of choice.

Attaching Patterns

Temporary-bond spray adhesive is the most common method used to attach patterns to blanks. Photocopy the pattern. Spray the adhesive on the back of the pattern, wait a few seconds, and then press the pattern down onto the blank. Rubber cement or glue sticks work similarly.

You can also use graphite or carbon transfer paper and a pencil. Choose a light-colored transfer paper for darker woods. Carbon paper costs less than graphite paper, but must be sanded off before finishing. Place the pattern on your blank and slip a sheet of transfer paper in between the pattern and the blank. Use a few pieces of blue painter's tape to hold the pattern and transfer paper in place. Trace around the pattern with a red pen so you know where you have traced.

Removing Patterns

Dampen the paper pattern with mineral spirits to aid in removal. A quick wipe of mineral spirits will remove most adhesives left behind on the wood. Commercial adhesive removers work, as well.

Blade Tension

Before inserting a blade, completely remove the tension. Then clamp both ends of the blade into the blade holders and adjust the tension. Push on the blade with your finger. It should flex no more than 1/8" (3mm) forward, backward, or side to side.

In general, it is better to make the blade too tight rather than too loose. A blade that does not have enough tension will wander. It will also flex from side to side, making for irregular or angled cuts. If you press too hard on a loose blade, it will likely snap.

A blade that has too much tension is more susceptible to breakage and tends to pull out of the blade holders.

Squaring Your Table

Most scroll saws have an adjustable table that allows you to make cuts at different angles. There are times when you want your saw set at an angle, but most cutting is done with the blade perpendicular to the table. If the table is even slightly off square, your cuts will be angled. This interferes with puzzle pieces, intarsia, segmentation, and many other scrolling projects.

The most common method for squaring your table is the small square method. Set the square flat on the saw table against a blade that has been inserted and tensioned. Adjust the table to form a 90° angle to the blade.

The cutting-through method is also popular. Saw through a piece of scrap wood at least ¾" (1.9cm) thick, and then check the angle of the cut using a square. Adjust the table until you get a perfectly square cut.

You can also use the kerf-test method. Take a 1¾" (4.5cm)-thick piece of scrap and cut about 1/16" (2mm)

into it. Stop the saw, and then spin the wood around to the back of the blade. If the blade slips easily into the kerf (the groove you just cut), the table is square. If it doesn't slide into the kerf, adjust the table and perform the test again until the blade slips in easily.

Safety

Take the time to properly prepare your workspace so that your scrolling experience is safe and enjoyable. Work in a well-ventilated space and surround your setup with good, even lighting. Always wear a dust mask and safety goggles, tie up long hair, and secure loose clothing before beginning a project in your shop. When using power tools such as drum sanders and band saws, employ a benchtop dust collector to help keep your work area clean and protect your lungs to ensure that you can scroll without difficulty for years to come.

Spalted Starfish

The name "starfish" describes an array of different creatures, each as brilliant and unearthly as the next. Relatives of the sand dollar and sea urchin, these saltwater dwellers are staples in "beachy" décor—what's more, they're a great way to use up small scraps of colorful or figured woods.

You can easily complete this piece in an afternoon, and it makes a great first intarsia project. This versatile design looks good in almost any size and color of wood.

I highly recommend selecting a piece of wood with attractive grain or figuring. This will make a huge difference in your final piece. For this project, I selected cypress and spalted figured maple.

Getting Started

Apply clear packaging tape to the surface of the wood. Cut the patterns, apply spray adhesive to the backs, and then position them on the wood.

1 **Cut the pieces.** Use a #7 reverse-tooth blade. Remove the pattern from the front and transfer the piece number to the back. Dry-assemble the pieces on a photocopy of the pattern.

2 **Mark where the adjoining pieces meet.** Use a pencil to make these marks on pieces 1, 3, and 5. Transfer these marks to the edges of the pieces.

3 **Rough shape piece 5.** Use a flex drum sander with an 80 to 120-grit sleeve. Pay attention to where it meets adjoining pieces. Replace the shaped piece to the pattern, and then make a pencil mark on the adjoining pieces so you know how much to sand the other pieces.

4 **Rough shape the remaining pieces.** Use the same technique and the flex drum sander.

5 **Add contour to the arms of the star.** Make the tip point up on some arms and make it point down on others. Add indents to some areas to make it look like the starfish is alive. Sand the pieces smooth with a 220-grit sleeve on the flex drum sander.

6 **Hand-sand each piece.** Fine tune the fit and soften any sharp edges. Remove any remaining pencil lines. Then buff the pieces with a 220-grit sanding mop.

7 **Dry-assemble the pieces.** Check the fit. Then edge glue the pieces together using wood glue. Allow the pieces to dry.

8 **Apply finish.** I used clear satin gel varnish, as I prefer the hand-rubbed look over a gloss or spray finish. It's a little extra work, but the results are worth it.

9 **Remove as much varnish as possible with paper towels.** Then use compressed air to remove the excess from tight areas. Wear safety glasses to keep the varnish out of your eyes. Use rubber-tipped dental tools and paper towels to get any remaining finish out of the cracks and crevices. Allow the finish to dry thoroughly.

10 **Trace the starfish onto the backing board.** Cut just inside the lines with a #2 blade. Lightly sand the edges with the mop sander to remove any fuzzies. Use a wide-tipped black marker to color the edges of the backing board to make it less visible. Apply a second coat of gel varnish to the starfish and allow it to dry according to the manufacturer's instructions.

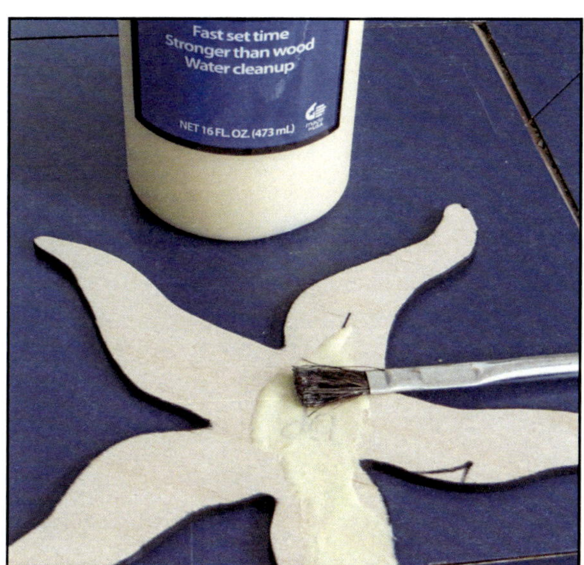

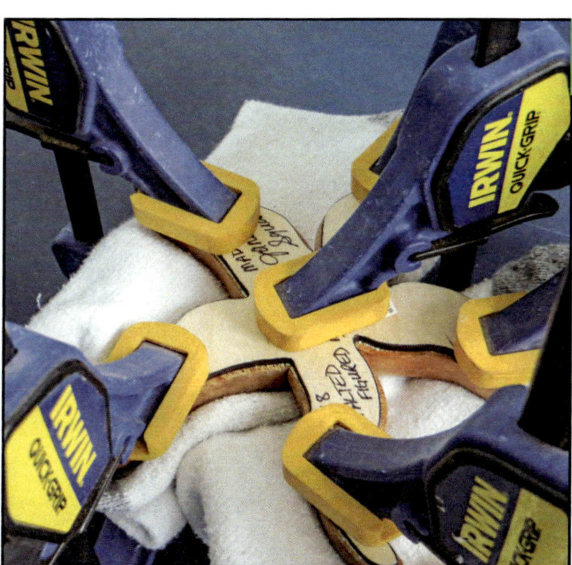

11 **Add a backer.** Apply wood glue to the top of the backing board. Position the starfish on the backing board and clamp it until the glue dries. Add a hanger to the back and sign your work.

Spalted Starfish Pattern

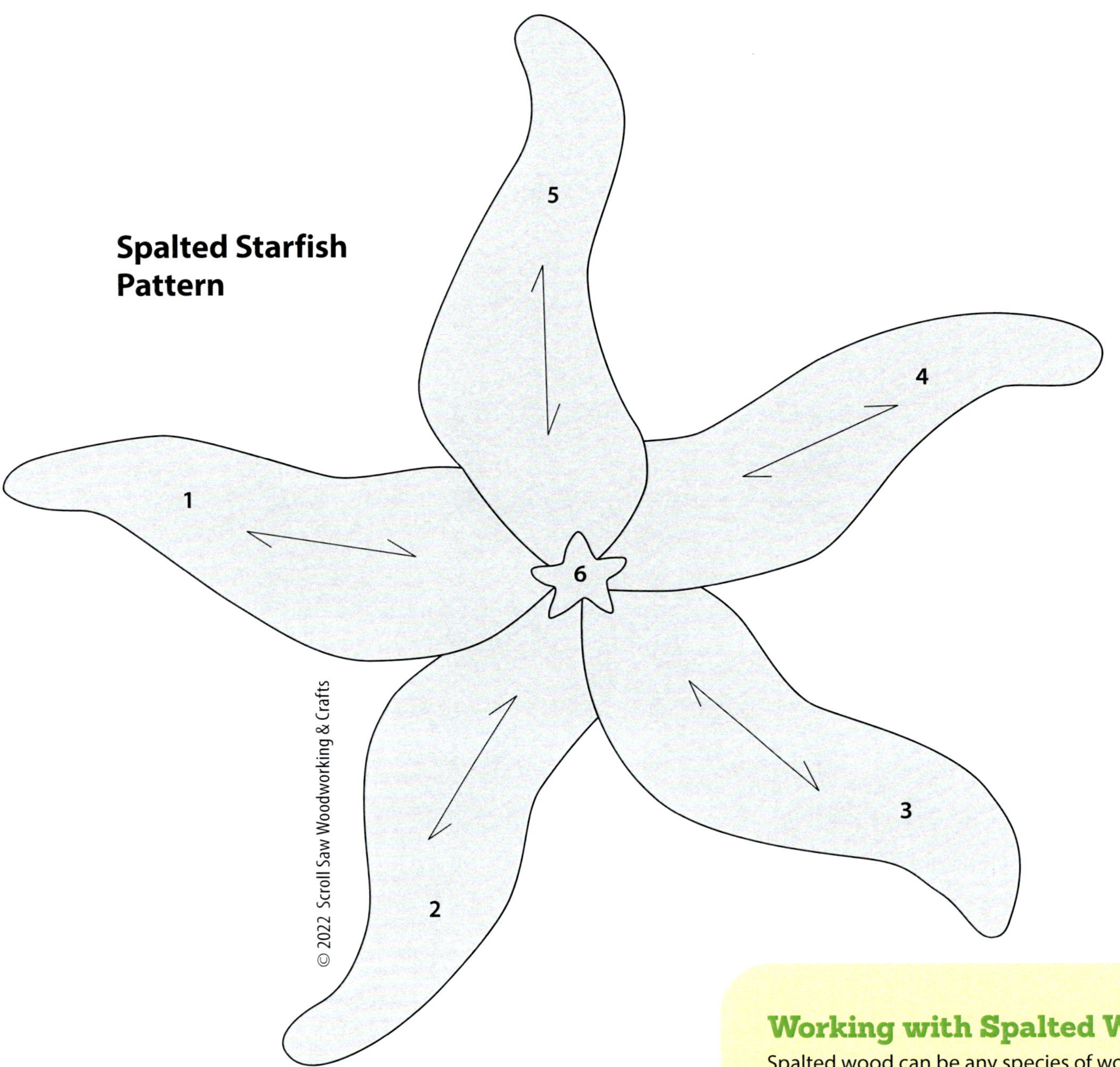

Materials & Tools

Materials
- Wood with an interesting grain, such as spalted maple, ¾" to 1" (1.9cm to 2.5cm) thick: starfish, 4" x 10" (10.2cm x 25.4cm)
- Baltic birch plywood, ⅛" (3mm) thick: backing board, 7" (17.8cm) square
- Tape: clear packaging
- Spray adhesive
- Sandpaper: 220-grit
- Glue: wood, cyanoacrylate (CA) (optional)
- Black marker
- Pencil
- Gel varnish: clear satin
- Paper towels
- Hanger
- Foam brush

Tools
- Scroll saw blades: #7, #2 reverse-tooth
- Sanders: flex drum; mop: 220-grit
- Sanding sleeves: 80 to 120-grit, 220-grit
- Dental tools: rubber-tipped
- Clamps
- Air compressor

The author used these products for the project. Substitute your choice of brands, tools, and materials as desired.

Working with Spalted Wood

Spalted wood can be any species of wood discolored slightly by a fungus. If you catch it before it's too rotten to work with, the color figure created by the fungus is beautiful. However, when working with spalted wood, be prepared for anything as far as grain, texture, and coloring go. Learn to embrace its imperfections since you never know what will show up as you sand your project. You must have some sort of breathing protection and dust collection; spalted wood dust can carry fungal spores that could damage your lungs. When working with spalted wood, note that you can run into a variety of wood densities throughout a single piece. This is caused by the varying stages of decay. If your wood is too soft, apply thin liquid cyanoacrylate (CA) glue and allow it to soak in. This will help stabilize the wood.

Smooth Seashell

Who doesn't love looking for seashells at the beach? Here's one you can create yourself—and if you're like me, hunting for interesting wood is as much fun as hunting for shells. By using quarter sawn sycamore or another uniquely grained wood, you can create a simple yet ornate shell to gift to an ocean-loving friend, or add to your own beach themed décor. It's a simple design to cut, but by spending a bit of extra time on the wood selection and shaping, you can create an ornate, high-quality piece of art.

Getting Started

Choose wood with a unique grain; I used sycamore and curly maple. As you contour these wood varities, the grain changes, so each piece will be truly different. Attach clear packing tape to the surface of the wood, and then apply the pattern to the tape using spray adhesive. *Note: I split the pattern into three separate sections—the main shell body (A), the hollow area (B), and the area framing the hollow (C). Cut the main body of the shell and the area framing the hollow from one piece of sycamore, and then divide it into the required number of segments. I used curly maple for the hollow area. This allowed for more grain variation, which gave the piece added interest. You could also just use a single 4" by 6" (10.2cm by 15.2cm) piece for the entire shell.*

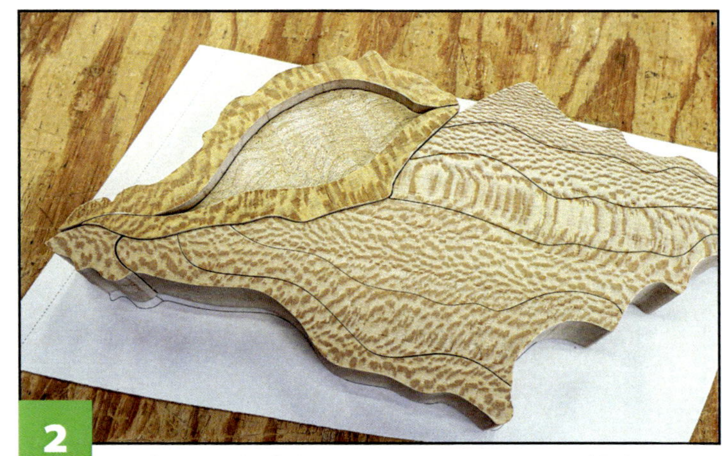

1 **Scroll the main pieces.** Cut the two frame pieces, the hollow area, and the perimeter of the main body of the shell using a #7 reverse-tooth blade.

2 **Cut the main body into segments.** Use a #2 or #3 blade. The smaller kerf will allow the pieces to reconnect with a tighter fit. Remove the patterns and reassemble the piece.

3 **Make the sanding shim.** Trace the perimeter of the shell onto a piece of ¼" (6mm) plywood, and then cut it on the scroll saw with the #2 or #3 blade. Attach the main part of the shell to the shim using double-sided tape. Roughly shape the overall body using a flex drum sander with 120-grit sandpaper.

4 **Rough shape the shell.** Draw the lines for the main shell sections to make the segments easier to see. Then, using a rotary tool with a medium-grit flame-shaped typhoon burr, rough shape the main shell body (A), leaving the hollow (B) and framing pieces (C) untouched for now. You want to create "hills and valleys" to simulate the highs and lows of the shell. Every shell is unique, so have fun with the shaping process on this one! Once you have established a consistent overall shape, continue with the individual segments of the body, adding even more interest. The end product should have a rippled effect resembling waves.

5 **Shape the concave hollow of the shell (B).** Lower the side closest to the main body to give the illusion that this area is descending down into the shell. Then shape the framing two pieces to align with the rest. Use the same tool as in Step 4.

6 **Refine the pieces.** Smooth out and eliminate the scratches with 120-grit paper in the flex drum sander. Using the edge of the sander helps to get into some of the tighter areas.

7 **Give the elements a final sand.** I used a combination of hand-sanding and a mop sander.

8 **Assemble the shell.** Place waxed paper over the extra pattern from Getting Started and assemble the shell on top of it. Look at the assembled shell from all angles. Once satisfied with the overall shape, edge-glue each piece to its neighbor. Allow the assembly to dry fully.

Finishing

Choose a finish. I prefer a satin gel varnish because it doesn't require sanding between coats and gives each piece a rich, hand-rubbed look. *Note: Always wear protective eyewear and gloves when applying finish.*

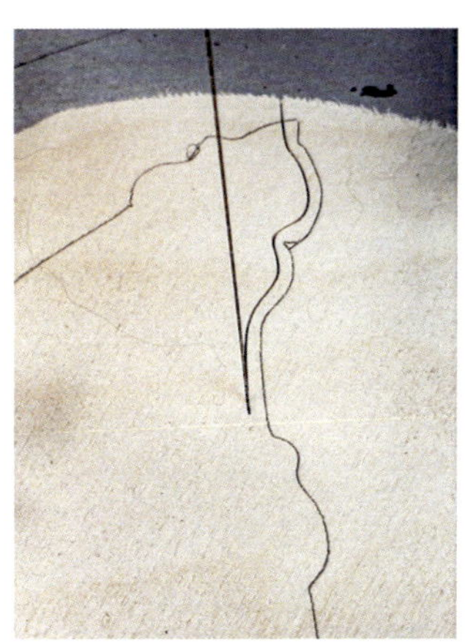

Apply the finish. Remove the excess with paper towels, and then use an air compressor, if desired, to get the remainder out of the cracks. A rubber-tipped dental tool is handy for getting into the grooves, as well. Let dry. Then add the backer. Trace the shell onto a piece of ⅛" (3mm)-thick Baltic birch plywood or your preferred material. Cut ¹⁄₁₆" to ⅛" (2mm to 3mm) inside the line and sand the backer with a mop sander. Glue the backer on, let dry, and sign your work. Add a hanger, if desired.

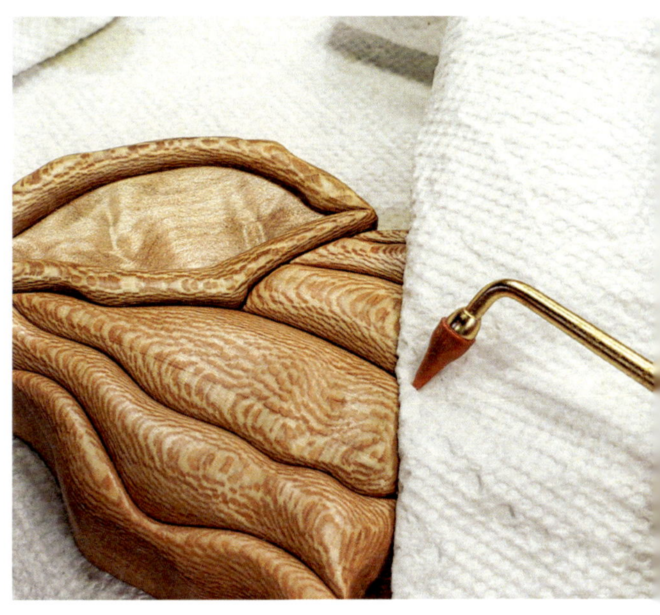

Smooth Seashell Pattern

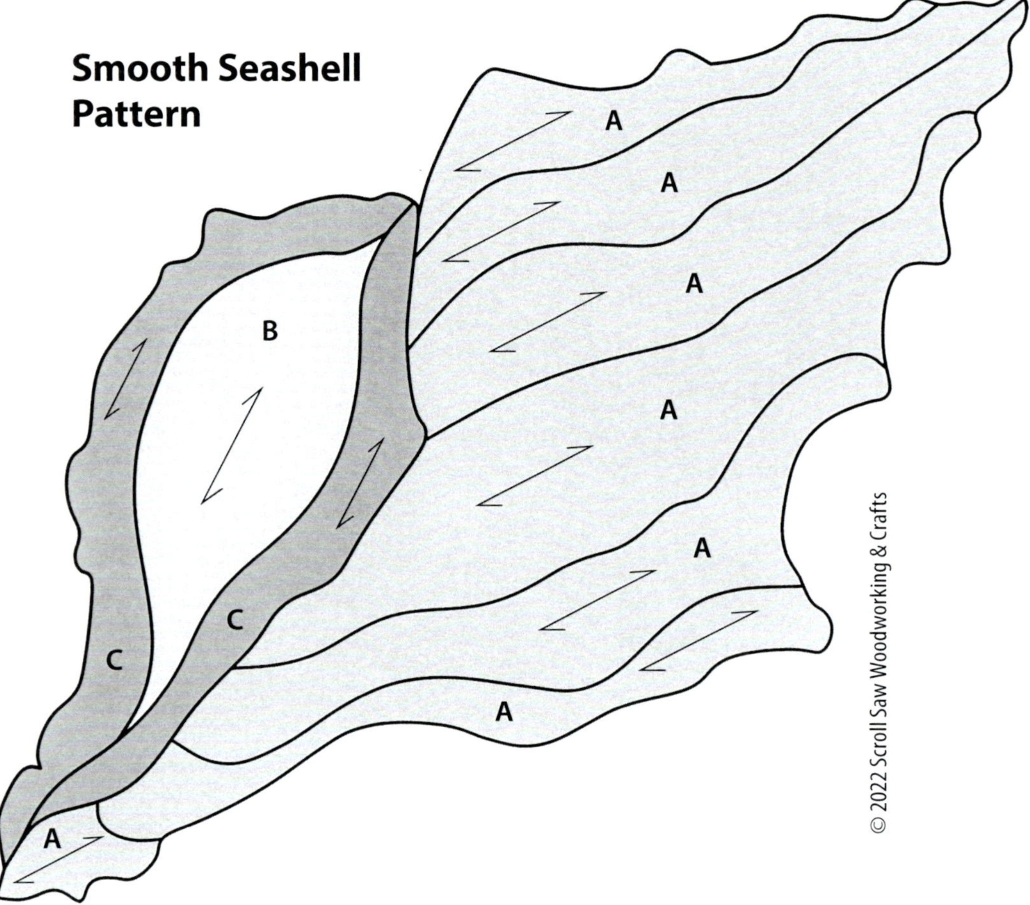

Materials & Tools

Materials
- Wood, such as quarter sawn sycamore, ¾" to 1" (1.9cm to 2.5cm) thick: shell, approx. 4" x 6" (10.2cm x 15.2cm)
- Wood, such as curly maple, ¾" to 1" (1.9cm to 2.5cm) thick: shell hollow, approx. 2" x 4" (5.1cm x 10.2cm)
- Wood, such as Baltic birch plywood, ⅛" (3mm) thick: backer, 4" x 6" (10.2cm x 15.2cm)
- Scrap plywood, ¼" (6mm) thick: sanding shim, 4" x 6" (10.2cm x 15.2cm)
- Tape: double-sided, clear packaging
- Spray adhesive
- Sandpaper: assorted grits
- Waxed paper
- Wood glue
- Finish: clear satin gel varnish
- Paper towels
- Hanger (optional)

Tools
- Scroll saw with blades: #2 or #3, #7 reverse-tooth
- Sander: mop; flex drum with 120 and 220-grit sandpaper
- Rotary tool with burr: medium-grit flame-shaped typhoon
- Dental tools: rubber-tipped
- Air compressor (optional)

The author used these products for the project. Substitute your choice of brands, tools, and materials as desired.

Cheeky Hermit Crab

Cut and shape a scuttling creature with as much sass as Sebastian

By Anatoly Obelets

Let this curious little hermit crab remind you of sunny days spent collecting pebbles at the beach. For an extra challenge, I've incorporated the Japanese *ukibori* (or pop-up carving) technique, which allows you to cover the exoskeleton with characteristic "freckles" as if by magic. You can apply this technique to other scrolled projects, too—for example, to make the tendons stand out on a hand, or to emphasize the ripples in a pool of water. The possibilities are endless!

Getting Started

Cut the pine to size and sand it smooth with 100 and then 150-grit sandpaper. Photocopy the pattern and transfer it to the blank; I use graphite paper and a pencil, but you can save time by attaching the design directly. Cover the wood with blue painter's tape and stick the pattern to the tape with spray adhesive. Attach the backer wood to the pine by wrapping clear packaging tape around the edges of the boards; you'll be removing it about halfway through the cutting process. Then drill the single blade-entry hole between the rightmost crab leg and the one below it.

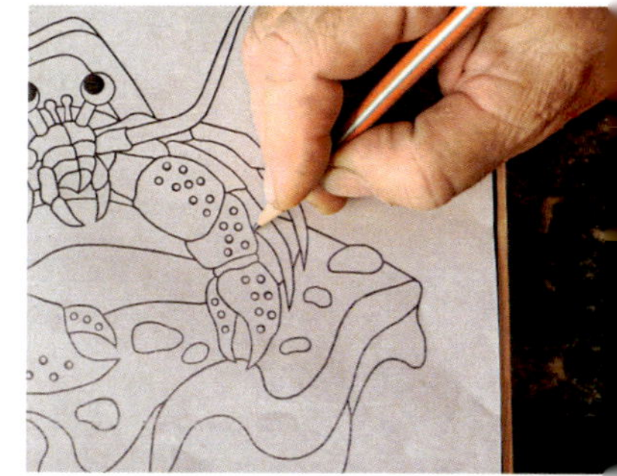

1 **Make the single interior cut.** Use a #7 blade or one of your choice. (I used a Pyrosegmentator—a precision cutting device I invented—but you can use a scroll saw.) Then begin to cut the perimeter of the scene.

2 **Carefully make the remaining cuts around the perimeter.** *Note: Keep in mind that you are cutting the plywood backer at the same time.* Separate the pine from the backer and set the backer aside.

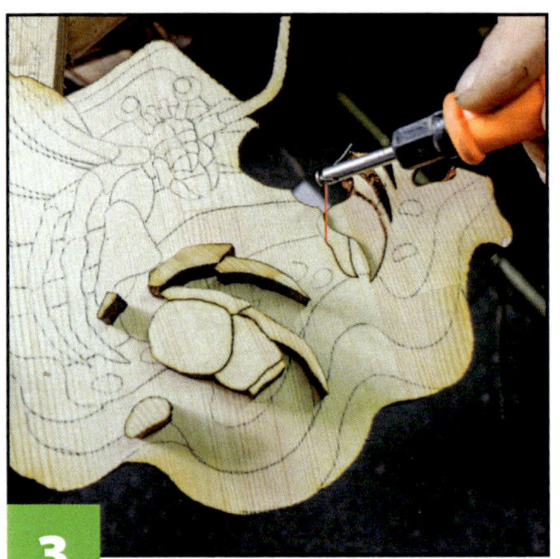 

3 **Cut the remaining pieces.** Cut them as you would a segmentation or puzzle. Use a #2 blade or one of your choice. Reassemble the pieces to prepare them for shaping.

4 **Shape the big claw.** Use a flex drum sander to round each element.

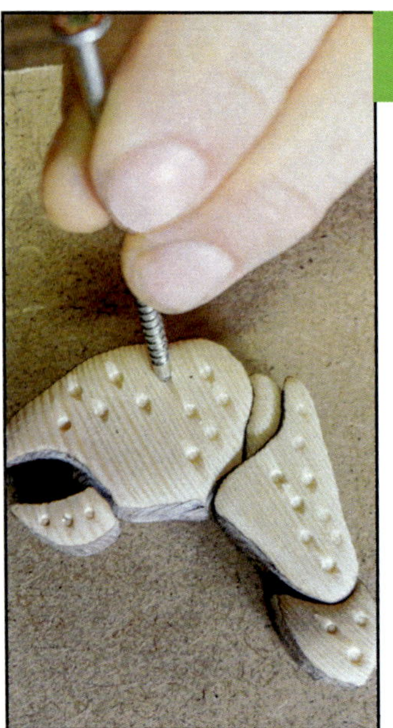 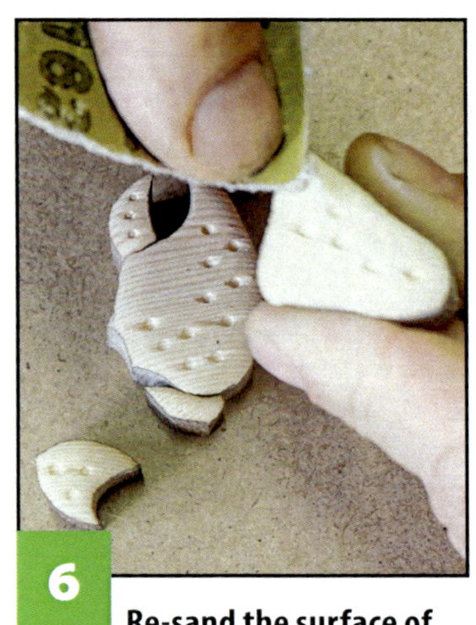 

5 **Add texture.** I applied the Japanese *ukibori* technique for visual interest. On the previously rounded surface of the claw, apply a series of shallow dents using a hammer and a metal rod. *Note: You can make your own by rounding off the end of a screw or nail with sandpaper.*

6 **Re-sand the surface of the claw.** When you are done, the surface should look almost entirely smooth again.

7 **Prepare a small bowl of hot water (122° Fahrenheit, 50° Celsius).** Apply the water to the surface of the claw with a small paintbrush. Shortly after, the dented areas will turn to raised "freckles." *Note: It's important to raise the wood soon after depressing it—if you wait until the next day, the technique won't work.*

8 **Apply a stain.** I used a cherry-colored stain for all of the crab's exoskeleton, but for now, just stain the big claw. Let dry, and then sand lightly with 220-grit sandpaper.

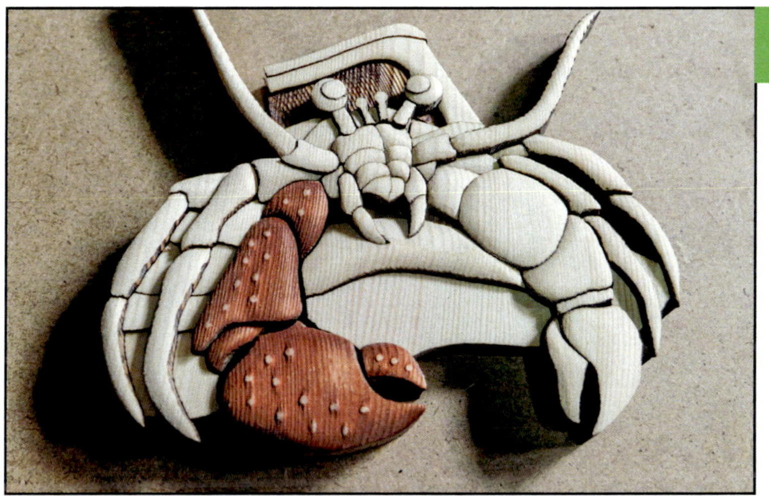

9 **Round the remaining details.** Use a combination of a palm sander and the flex drum sander. The crab and shell should be thickest, followed by the waves and rocks. The sand will be the lowest layer, giving the final piece depth and dimension. In this design, I waited until the crab was completely shaped before moving on to the surrounding scene; this ensures that I can adjust the thickness of the other pieces based on the final thickness of the crab. Then, once all of the pieces are shaped, apply the *ukibori* technique from Steps 5-7 to the second claw.

10 **Color the remaining pieces.** The advantage of a light wood like pine is that many colors will work for this project. I went with bold alcohol-based stains and dyes, but you could use something more subtle. Once the stains or dyes have dried, gently sand along the edges to create a faded, antiqued look. Then glue the pieces to the backer, one by one. Finish with clear matte varnish, let dry, and display as desired; I added a hanger to the back.

Materials
- Wood, such as pine, ¾" (1.9cm) thick: crab scene, 8⅝" x 11" (21.9cm x 27.9cm)
- Plywood or tempered hardboard, ⅛" (3mm) thick: backer, 8⅝" x 11" (21.9cm x 27.9cm)
- Tape: blue painter's, clear packaging
- Spray adhesive
- Graphite paper (optional)
- Pencil
- Sandpaper: assorted grits to 220
- Hot water
- Assorted alcohol-based stains and dyes, such as fireside cherry, golden pine, light fern, light oak, mahogany, and teak
- Varnish: clear matte
- Wood glue

- Hanger: D-ring (optional)
- Small bowl

Tools
- Scroll saw with blades: #2, #7 reverse-tooth
- Drill with bit: ³⁄₆₄" (1.2mm)-dia.
- Sanders: palm, flex drum
- Metal rods or old screws or nails, slightly rounded: ¹⁄₁₆" to ⅛" (2mm to 3mm)-dia.
- Small hammer
- Clamps
- Paintbrushes: assorted

The author used these products for the project. Substitute your choice of brands, tools, and materials as desired.

Cheeky Hermit
Crab Pattern
© 2022 Scroll Saw Woodworking & Crafts

Stylized Seahorse

By Patrick Wayner

My family and I love the beach. And if you're like us, you know the worst part is having to leave. I came up with this seahorse project to bring some ocean vibes back home with us (minus the pocket full of sand). The goal was to achieve a weathered look, similar to something that might hang at your favorite beach house.

I chose design elements like golden wave art paper and metallic splatter to mimic the sun's shimmer. The yellows of an early sunrise and the blues and grays of a beach night became my color palette.

The seahorse's curvy shape makes this project a fun ride on the scroll saw. The design elements and color pattern leave room for creative interpretation, so you can adapt them based on personal preference.

Getting Started

Photocopy the pattern and prepare the stock. You'll cut the shaped pieces from ½" (1.3cm) MDF and the backer from ¼" (6mm). Stack the two pieces, and then attach them together using your preferred method; I used a 23-gauge pin nailer with ¼" (6mm) brads, placing a pin in each of the four corners (outside the pattern lines). You could also secure the edges using cyanoacrylate (CA) glue or clear packaging tape. Cover the surface of the stack with contact paper or painter's tape. Then apply the pattern to the surface of the paper or attach using spray adhesive. I also apply a layer of clear packaging tape over the entire surface of the blank to reduce the odds of the blade burning the wood, but you can leave this step out, if desired.

1 Cut the perimeter of the seahorse. Use a scroll saw with a #3 reverse-tooth blade. *Note: This is a very curvy pattern. You may want to reduce your scroll saw speed to 80%.* Separate the two MDF layers and set the backer aside.

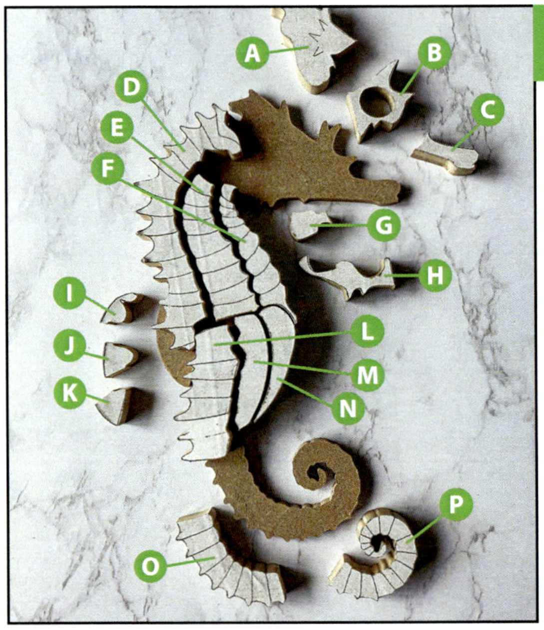

2 Drill the pilot hole for the eye. Then cut out the eyeball area on the scroll saw and cut the seahorse into smaller sections. I cut the chest and belly areas down the two vertical lines (forming sections DEF, LMN), and then cut the tail area into two smaller sections (O,P). Place the pieces back on the backer as you go to keep them organized.

3 Create the levels. For each main body section (head, neck and chest, belly, and tail), leave the first piece to the left alone. Then reduce depth in ⅛" (3mm) increments from the following two pieces (center and right) on a belt sander with an 80-grit sanding belt. This will give the seahorse more dimension and interest.

4 Separate the remaining sections. As before, place the pieces on the base as you cut them. Remove the pattern as you go.

STAYING ORGANIZED

Organization is key when you're cutting smaller pieces. It is difficult to remember how the pattern goes back together if the pieces get out of order. Always use your backer or a second copy of the pattern to help keep the smaller pieces together. If desired, you could also stick them to a piece of painter's tape.

5 **Shape the pieces.** Arrange the unshaped elements in order with about a ½" (1.3cm) space between the pieces. Using the belt sander with a 120-grit belt, begin to round over the edges on the larger pieces. It is best to pull the pieces toward you in a sweeping motion on each edge. Repeat this step on each edge of every piece of the seahorse. Once you reach the lower tail section, you may want to use a rotary tool with a 120-grit sanding drum to round the edges. The smaller the piece, the harder it will be to do on the belt sander. Once the edges are roughly rounded over, hand-sand them with 400-grit sandpaper to refine the contours. Remove excess dust with a tack cloth. Dry-fit the pieces and make any necessary adjustments.

PAINTING & FINISHING

6 **Apply art paper to the desired pieces.** *Note: You can buy patterned art paper online or at popular craft store chains. Alternatively, use old maps or interesting book covers for this step. Have fun with it!* Using the pieces you want to cover as a template, cut around each one with a utility blade, or trace around the pieces and cut along the lines with scissors. Then apply a liberal amount of craft glue to the tops of the pieces with a flat head brush. Wait a few minutes for the glue to become tacky, or speed up the process slightly with a blow dryer. Tightly press the art paper onto each desired piece, and then lightly sand the edges of the paper with 400-grit sandpaper to help fuse them to the wood. Apply one more coat of craft glue to the top and let dry. Place the pieces back on the base.

7 **Add color.** I recommend choosing five different colors to help define the sections. I used a mixture of latex house paint and artist acrylics. Apply the paint to the pieces as desired, using an acrylic ¼" (6mm) filbert brush. Once dry, distress the edges with 400-grit sandpaper to make the facets pop.

8 **Add the painted details.** Embellish the painted pieces by splitting the elements into sections and applying different techniques to each (see Sidebar on page 19).

9 **Assemble the project.** First, make sure there is no paint on the bottom of your pieces (sand if needed). Then attach the pieces to the backer using cyanoacrylate (CA) or wood glue, starting with the head. A little goes a long way here, so don't overdo it. Let the head area dry, and then attach the adjacent sections, moving progressively across the body a little at a time. Use the curves of the edges on the base to make sure your pieces are lined up.

10 **Apply a finish.** I used several light coats of a clear polycrylic, letting the finish dry fully between applications. Glue in the eyeball. *Note: I used a clear taxidermy eyeball because it allowed me to paint the area around the pupil any color I chose. However, you could use a pre-colored glass eye, if desired.* Add a hanger to the back, if desired.

TIP

USING ACCELERATOR

You can use an accelerator to speed up glue drying time. The trade-off for this method is that the glue will dry very quickly, so work fast.

Materials & Tools

Materials
- Wood of choice, such as MDF, ¼" (6mm) thick: seahorse segments, 5½" x 10" (14cm x 25.4cm)
- Wood of choice, such as MDF, ½" (1.3cm) thick: backer, 5½" x 10" (14cm x 25.4cm)
- Tape: painter's, clear packaging
- Contact paper
- Spray adhesive
- Glue: cyanoacrylate (CA) or wood
- Glue accelerator, such as Starbond (optional)
- Sandpaper: assorted grits to 400
- Tack cloth
- Craft glue, such as Mod Podge®
- Latex house paint
- Acrylic paints, such as Liquitex™: cobalt green, light blue violet, Naples yellow hue, neutral gray, titanium white
- Metallic paint, such as Montana™ Liquid Gold: silver
- Glass eye: clear back, ⅝" (16mm)-dia.
- Art pattern paper of choice
- Old maps or book covers (optional)
- Clear polycrylic spray, such as Minwax®
- Hanger (optional)

Tools
- Scroll saw with blades: #3 reverse-tooth
- Drill press with bit: ⅛" (3mm)-dia.
- Pin nailer with brads: ¼" (6mm)
- Belt sander: 6" (15.2cm) with 80 and 120-grit belts
- Utility knife
- Rotary tool with sanding drum: 120-grit
- Acrylic paintbrushes: ¼" (6mm) filbert, ½" (13mm) flat head
- Liner brush: 0
- Blow dryer or heat gun (optional)
- Scissors

The author used these products for the project. Substitute your choice of brands, tools, and materials as desired.

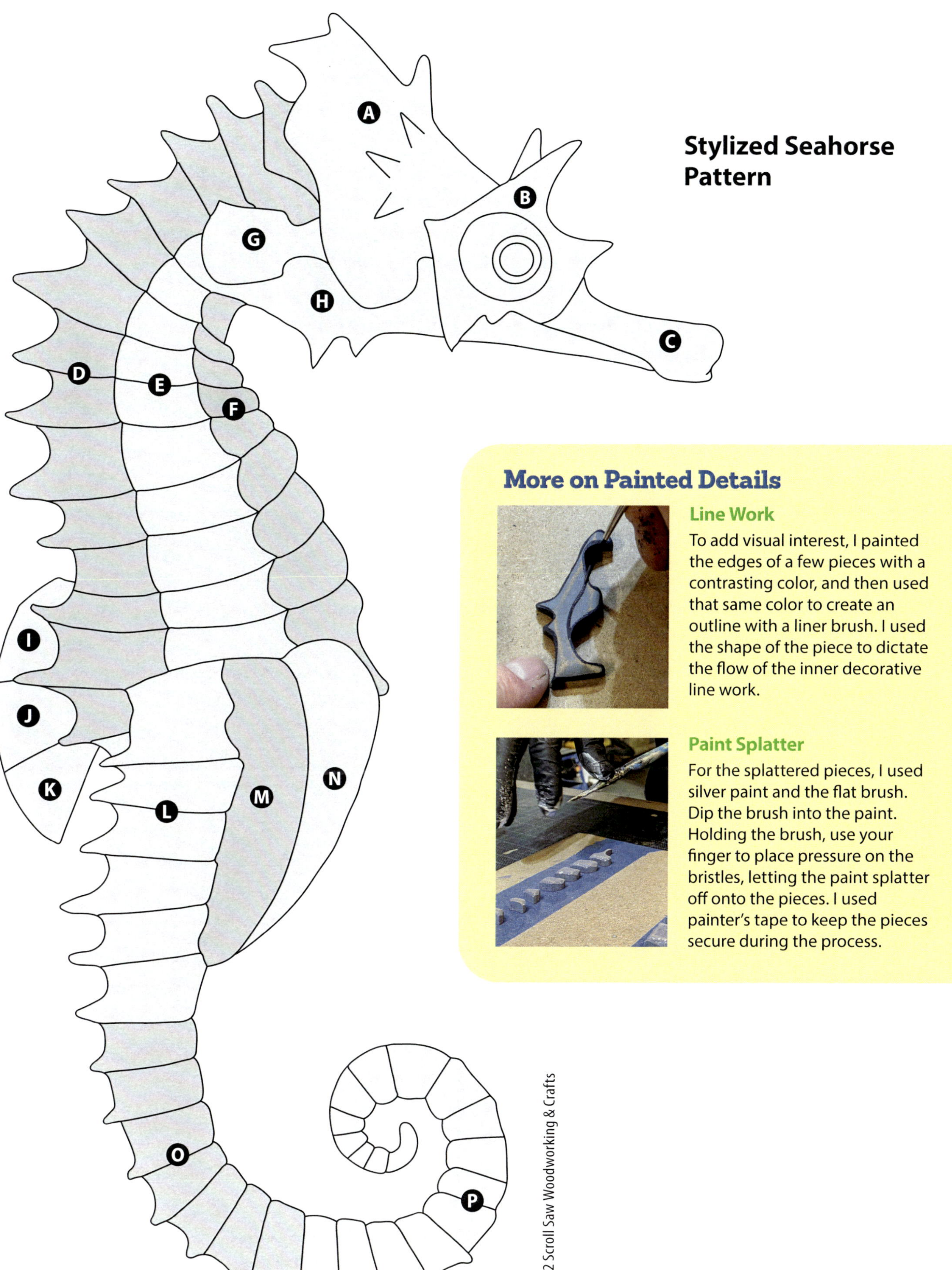

Stylized Seahorse Pattern

More on Painted Details

Line Work

To add visual interest, I painted the edges of a few pieces with a contrasting color, and then used that same color to create an outline with a liner brush. I used the shape of the piece to dictate the flow of the inner decorative line work.

Paint Splatter

For the splattered pieces, I used silver paint and the flat brush. Dip the brush into the paint. Holding the brush, use your finger to place pressure on the bristles, letting the paint splatter off onto the pieces. I used painter's tape to keep the pieces secure during the process.

Perching Pelican

Seaside scene is a fun nautical accent

By Kathy Wise

This content pelican is sitting atop a piling at the water's edge, waiting for its next meal. The design brings back fond memories of vacations at the seashore and is a great addition to beach house décor.

I used bird's eye maple for the pelican's body because the grain pattern resembles feathers. I also used cherry, black walnut, yellowheart, sycamore, bocote, wenge, and ebony. You can add optional details on the sycamore rope with a woodburner.

Getting Started

Make six copies of the pattern and keep a master copy for later use. Cut and group the pattern pieces together by color. Apply spray adhesive to the back of the pattern pieces, attach them to the shiny side of a piece of clear contact paper, and then cut the pattern pieces apart. The contact paper makes it easy to remove the patterns from the wood without leaving a sticky residue. The contact paper also lubricates the scroll saw blade as you cut the pieces. Plane any wood that is not flat before attaching the patterns to the stock. Attach a full-size pattern to a piece of thin plywood or hardboard to use as a backing board and assembly board.

CUTTING THE PIECES

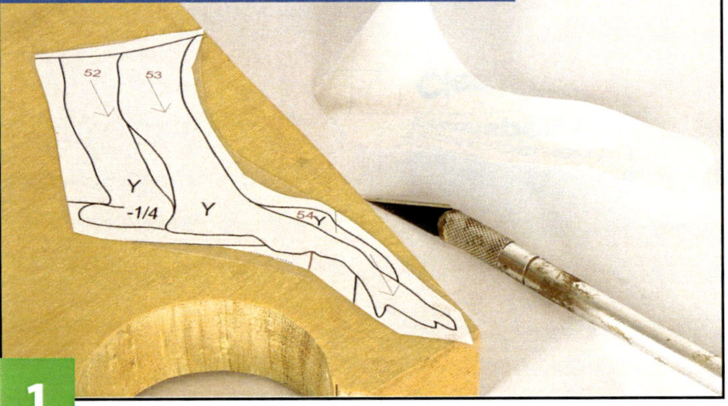

1 **Attach the patterns.** Peel and stick the pattern pieces onto the wood. Align the grain direction according to the arrows on the pattern pieces. Cut the large pieces into smaller manageable pieces. Use a small square to check a cut piece to make sure your blade is square to the table.

2 **Cut the pieces.** Use a #5 reverse-tooth blade. Cut the individual feathers from the wing section with a #2 or #3 blade. This method gives you a larger piece of wood to hold as you cut. Number the bottom of each cut piece with a pencil.

3 **Cut the riser for the tip of the wing.** Cut or plane a piece of the same wood you used for the wing to ½" (1.3cm)-thick. Trace the tip of the wing onto the riser and cut along the traced line. Glue the wing piece to the riser, and then sand the edges so it appears to be one piece.

4 **Cut the other risers.** Use the pattern as a guide to cut ½" (1.3cm)-thick risers for the rest of the wing. Glue the riser to the bottom of the main wing section, adjacent to the riser made from the same wood. Do not glue the small feathers to the riser yet. Cut a ¼" (6mm)-thick riser for the cheek area.

"

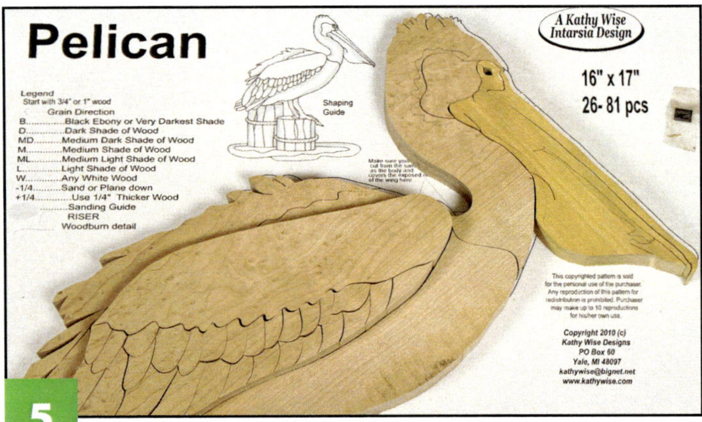

5 **Dry-assemble the pieces.** Place the cut pieces and risers in place on the pattern taped to the backing board. Check the fit and grain direction of the pieces. If there are major problems in the fit, color, or grain direction, cut new pieces now. You can fine-tune the fit of the pieces later.

SHAPING THE PIECES

6 **Establish the basic contours.** Sand the shaded areas indicated on the shaping guide. I used a pneumatic drum sander, but you can use other drum sanders or a rotary-power carver equipped with sanding drums, if desired. I wear rubber fingertips to protect fingers while sanding.

7 **Shape the lowest pieces.** Lower the water pieces, and then mark the height of the water on the pilings. Lower the pilings, but do not go lower than the pencil mark. Shape the rope, keeping it higher than the pilings. Replace the pieces back into the project often.

8 **Shape the pilings.** Sand a slight curve on each piece of the piling. Remove the rope section and line up the top and bottom pieces of the piling to make sure you are sanding them to the same level.

9 **Shape the tight curves.** I used a ½" (13mm)-dia. sanding drum in a rotary-power carver or an oscillating spindle sander with a ½" (13mm)-dia. drum to round the inside of tight curves, such as the curves in the bottom water pieces.

10 **Shape the feet.** Mark the level for the feet, keeping them thicker than the pilings. Sand and shape the feet using the lines as a guide. Make sure the foot that appears farther from the viewer is thinner or lower than the other foot.

11 **Shape the wings.** Mark the edges of the wings where they meet the lower body. Do not sand lower than this mark. Sand a sharp bevel onto each feather so they appear to fit under the adjacent ones. Round the outside edges of the wing sections and each feather.

12 **Shape the head, neck, and body.** Glue the cheek area to the riser and keep that section higher than the surrounding pieces. Round the body and neck. Sketch in guidelines and shape the beak. Use a rotary-power carver or carving tools to add the feather details to the head. Round the eye and fit it into the corresponding hole.

13 **Finish sanding the pieces.** Dry-assemble the project and check for overall fit and flow. Make any necessary adjustments, and then buff the pieces with a 220-grit sanding mop. The mop works quickly, fits into the curves and crevices, and gives the pieces a beautiful sheen.

ASSEMBLING

14 **Assemble the pelican in sections.** Use cyanoacrylate (CA) glue to tack the sections together. This keeps the pieces from shifting around as you glue them to the backing board. Glue together the head and neck; the top of the back and upper wing; the water, feet, and pilings; and the back feathers. Do not glue the small feathers together.

15 **Assemble the wing feathers.** Assemble all of the sections on the backing board. Remove the wing feathers in sections and keep them in the proper order. Spread five-minute epoxy on the riser. With the riser in position, quickly place the feathers in position and adjust them to fit evenly before the epoxy dries. Tack all of the parts of the pelican together with CA glue.

16 **Attach the backing board.** Trace the outline of the assembled project onto the backing board. Cut 1/16" (2mm) inside the line. Apply wood glue to the back of the project and use dots of CA glue between the wood glue. Apply CA glue accelerator to the backing board and press the project onto the backing board until the CA glue sets.

> **TIP**
>
> ### BETTER GLUE ADHESION
>
> *Use a stationary drum sander to sand the bottom of your project flat after you tack the pieces together. The flat back will sit perfectly on the backing board and give you a solid glue joint.*

17 **Apply the finish.** Because this project has many small pieces, I use a clear satin spray varnish finish. Follow the manufacturer's directions and apply two coats of finish, allowing the varnish to dry thoroughly between coats. Apply clear gloss finish to the eyes for a lifelike look. Attach your hanger of choice to the back.

Materials

- Medium-dark wood, such as boeate, ¾" (1.9cm) thick: piling, 5" x 6" (12.7cm x 15.2cm)
- Medium figured wood, such as wavy maple, ½" (1.3cm) thick: water, 4" x 16" (10.2cm x 40.6cm)
- Black-stained wood or ebony, ½" (1.3cm) thick: eye, 1" (2.5cm) square
- Light wood, such as sycamore, 1" (2.5cm) thick: rope, 3" x 6" (7.6cm x 15.2cm)
- Yellow wood, such as yellowheart, 1" (2.5cm) thick: beak, 5" x 9" (12.7cm x 22.9cm)
- Dark wood, such as wenge, ¾" (1.9cm) thick: piling, 6" x 7" (15.2cm x 17.8cm)
- Light wood, such as bird's eye maple, 1" (2.5cm) thick: body, 9" x 19" (22.9cm x 48.3cm)
- Plywood or tempered hardboard, ¼" (6mm) thick: backing board, 14" x 16" (35.6cm x 40.6cm)
- Plywood, ½" (13mm) thick: risers, 5" x 10" (12.7cm x 25.4cm)
- Pencil
- Five-minute epoxy
- Contact paper: clear
- Spray adhesive
- Clear satin spray varnish
- Clear gloss finish (eyes)
- Rags
- Hanger
- Glue: cyanoacrylate (CA), wood
- Glue accelerator
- Dark stain or black spray paint (optional to paint edges of backing board)

Tools

- Scroll saw with blades: #2 or #3, #5 reverse-tooth blades
- Sanders: pneumatic drum, spindle, stationary drum (optional)
- Sanding mop: 220-grit
- Rotary tool with bits: assorted sanding drums
- Carving tools (optional)
- Woodburner (optional)
- Small square
- Rubber fingertips

The author used these products for the project. Substitute your choice of brands, tools, and materials as desired.

Perching Pelican Pattern

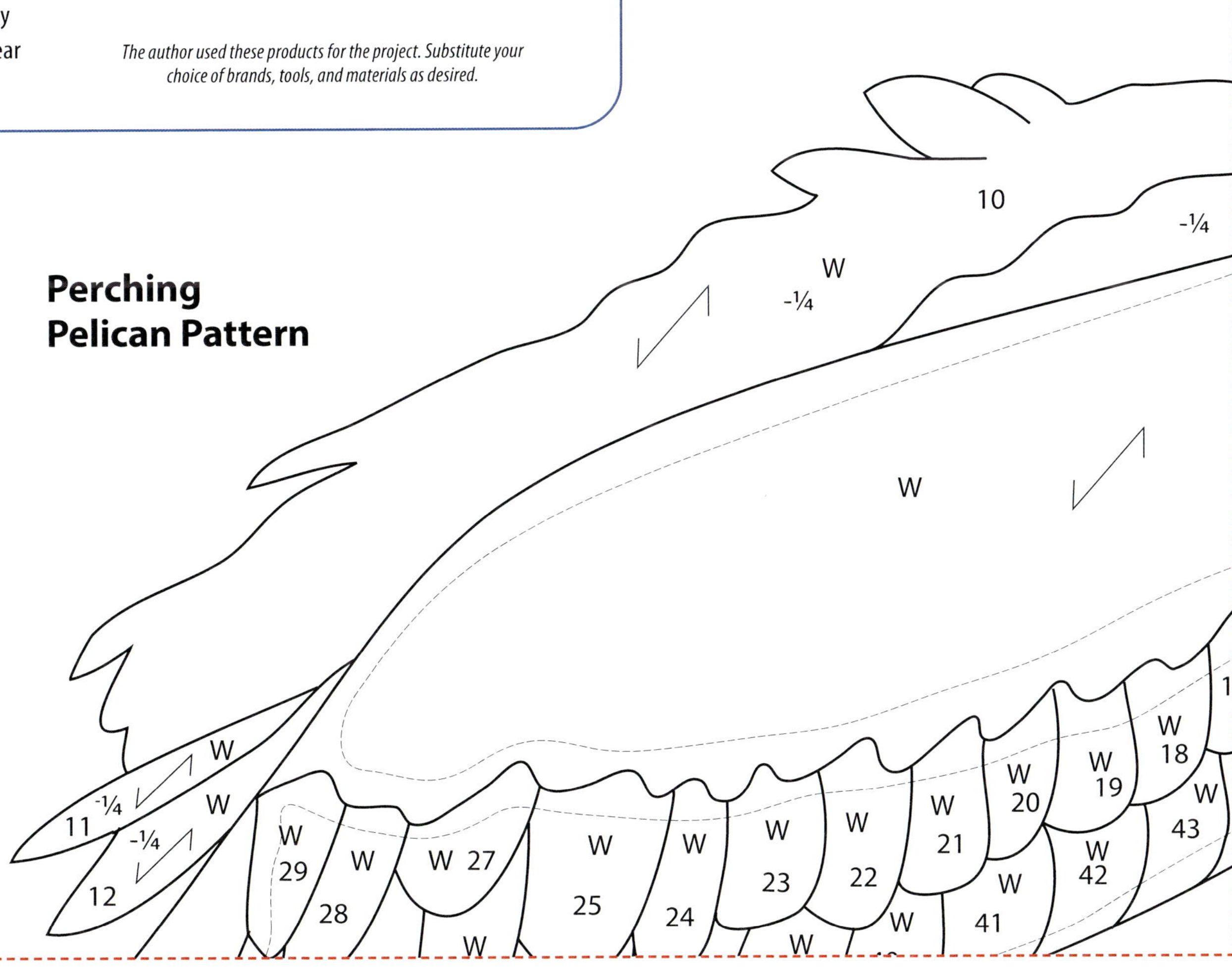

Perching Pelican Patterns
3
Riser +¼
B 1 2
W 4
Y
5 Y
6 Y
7
Y
W
Make sure your riser is cut from the same wood as the body and covers the exposed end of the wing here
9 W
8
Riser +½
M
13 W
W
W 16
W 15
14 W
W
7
45 W
W 44
W

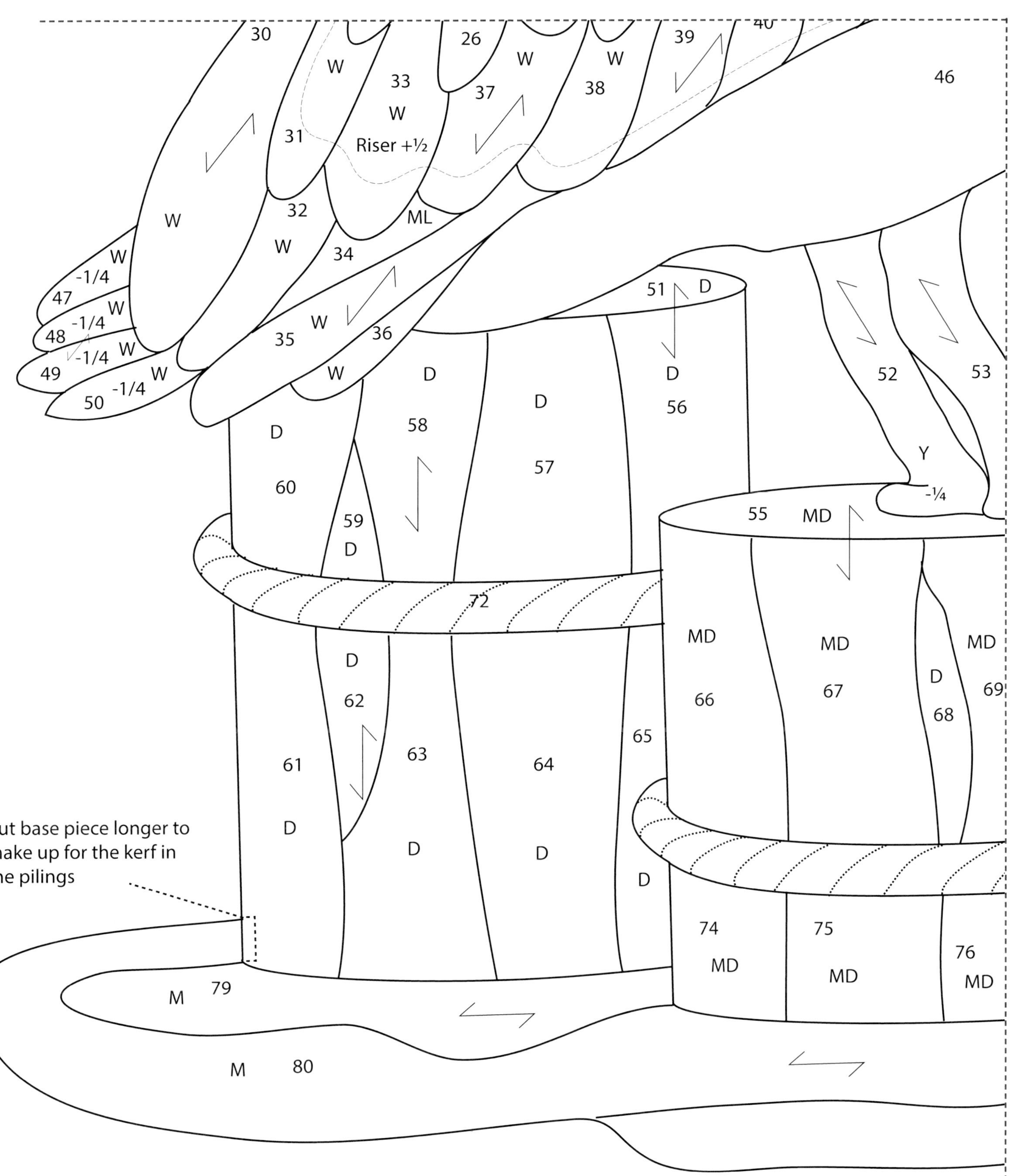

30
W
33
26
W
W
39
40
46
31
W
Riser +½
37
38
32
W
34
ML
W
W
-1/4
47
W
-1/4
48
W
-1/4
49
W
50
-1/4
35
W
36
W
51
D
D
D
58
D
56
D
57
52
53
Y
-¼
60
59
D
55
MD
72
MD
MD
MD
D
66
67
68
69
D
62
61
63
64
65
MD
D
D
D
Cut base piece longer to
make up for the kerf in
the pilings
D
74
75
76
MD
M
79
MD
MD
MD
M
80

Perching Pelican Patterns

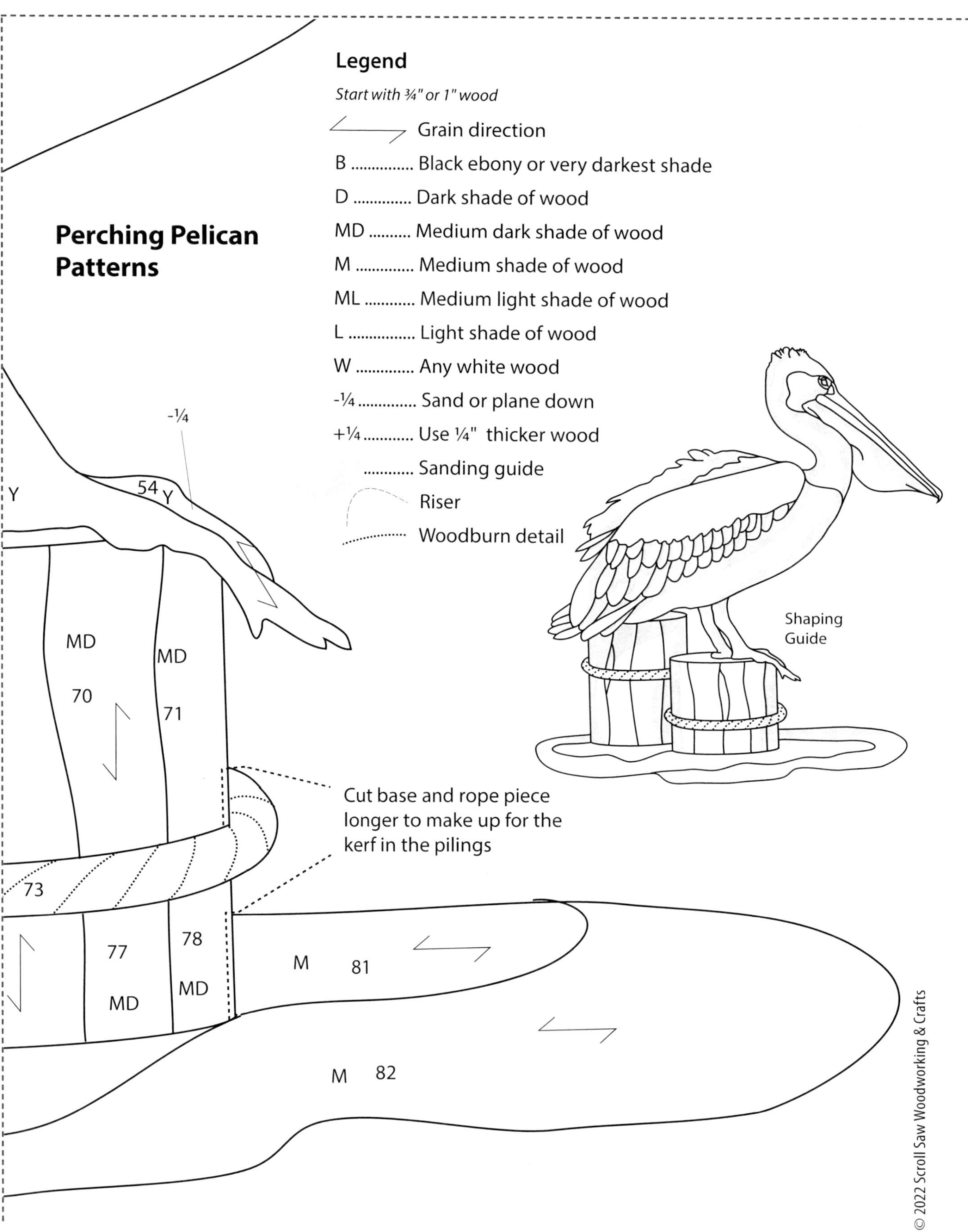

Nantucket Lighthouse

Create a classic intarsia look with stains

By Frank Droege

Although I can't claim this technique as my own, I do enjoy making "painted pictures" using my scroll saw, soft woods, a sander, and some stains. Soft woods are readily available and, best of all, a lot less expensive than exotic woods. This is a great project for anyone who wants to try an intarsia-like technique without spending a fortune on wood.

Getting Started

Make four copies of the pattern. Number each piece on two copies. Cut each piece in the pattern with a knife, such as a small box knife or an X-ACTO® knife. Glue the pattern to the wood with temporary-bond spray adhesive. Note the arrows on the pattern. They indicate how to position the pattern relative to the grain of the wood.

Cutting and Sanding

Cut out the patterns. I use #2 reverse-tooth blades since they do not leave a burr on the bottom of the piece. Do not rush the cut. Take it easy and let the blade do the work. The extra time you spend now is made up when you do not have to do any extra fitting of the pieces. After cutting the pieces, make sure you mark the number on the bottom of each piece. After marking the bottom, remove the paper from the wood.

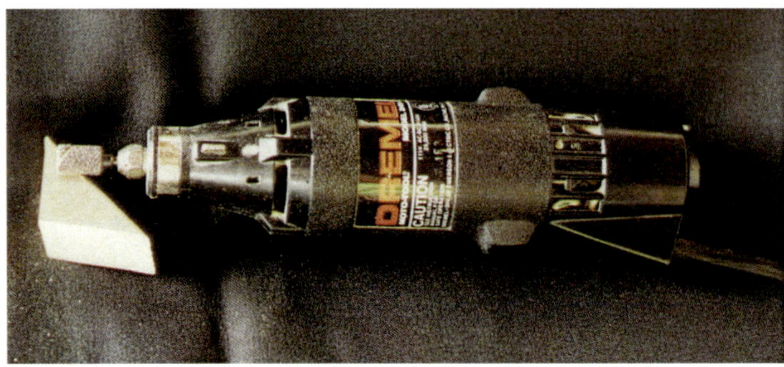

Round the edges to a ¹⁄₁₆" (2mm)-dia. radius using a rotary tool and a ⅛" (3mm) diamond burr. Remove any marks or spray adhesive with 180-grit sandpaper. Assemble to see if everything fits properly. You may need to make the pieces a little bit smaller. Depending on how much excess wood you need to remove, you might want to use the diamond burr, a file, or maybe even the scroll saw. Raise and lower pieces. The door area will sit higher than the main lighthouse, and the lighthouse and ground will sit higher than the sky.

Finishing

Stain the pieces. Apply the stain with a brush. After waiting a few minutes to let the stain penetrate the wood, take a soft rag and wipe off the excess. The amount of wiping you do will affect how much grain shows. Make sure all visible areas are stained. Let dry.

Assemble the parts by gluing the edges together, making sure no glue gets on the top surface. Do the gluing on a piece of waxed paper over the pattern. Allow the glue to dry for eight to 24 hours.

Once dry, peel the waxed paper from the wood. Glue the whole assembly to a ⅛" or ¼" (3mm to 6mm) backer board, and then clamp it all around the edges. Give the work two coats of clear shellac, letting the coats dry between applications. Lightly sand. Apply two coats of water-soluble satin varnish, and lightly sand between coats. Add a sawtooth hanger to the back and display.

TIP

CREATING LEVELS

To raise a piece, simply glue a shim of the appropriate thickness to the piece. To lower, you'll need to remove wood. If the piece is less than two inches, you can do this on the scroll saw. If the piece is larger than two inches, you can use a band saw, if you have one. If not, you can break or cut the piece, trim it down, and then glue the pieces together again.

Materials
- Soft wood, such as soft pine or white cedar, ¾" (1.9cm) thick: 9" x 12" (22.9cm x 30.5cm)
- Backing board, ⅛" to ¼" (3mm to 6mm) thick: 9" x 12" (22.9cm x 30.5cm)
- Sandpaper: 180-grit
- Waxed paper
- Soft rag
- Temporary bond spray adhesive
- Water-based stains: colors of choice
- Water-soluble stain varnish
- Shellac: clear
- Sawtooth hanger

Tools
- Scroll saw with blades: #2 reverse-tooth
- Band saw (optional)
- Small box knife or X-ACTO® knife
- Rotary tool with bit: ⅛" (3mm) diamond-coated burr
- Clamps
- File
- Foam brush

The author used these products for the project. Substitute your choice of brands, tools, and materials as desired.

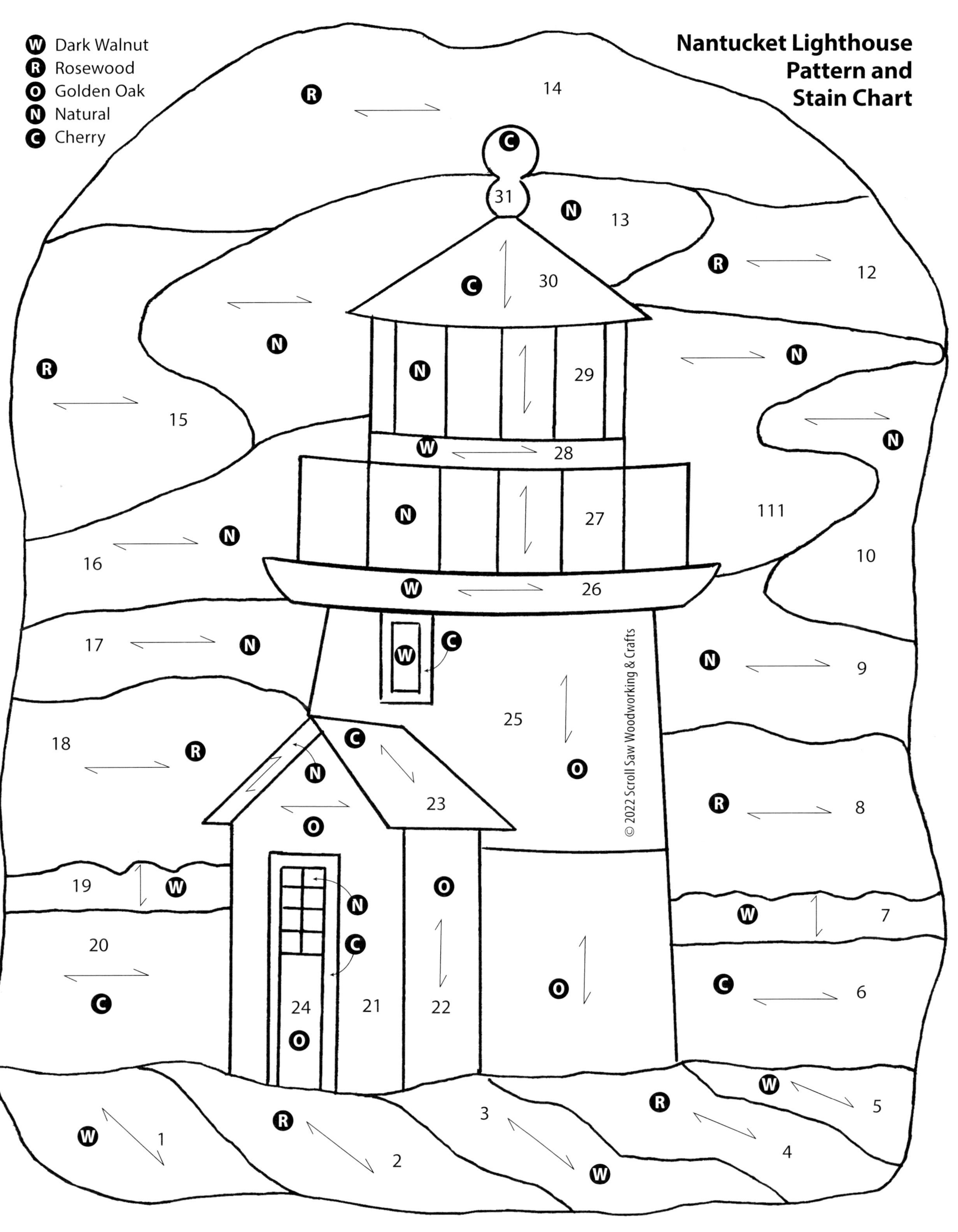

W Dark Walnut
R Rosewood
O Golden Oak
N Natural
C Cherry
Nantucket Lighthouse
Pattern and
Stain Chart
© 2022 Scroll Saw Woodworking & Crafts
1
2
3
4
5
6
7
8
9
10
111
12
13
14
15
16
17
18
19
20
21
22
23
24
25
26
27
28
29
30
31

Picasso Triggerfish

By Brad and Hazel Eklund

When it comes to eclectic style, nothing beats the Picasso triggerfish, lagoon triggerfish, or, as Hawaiians say, *humuhumunukunukuapua'a*. No matter what you call it, this colorful tropical fish, named for its "painted" look, is a star. Not only can you impress friends and family by making this vibrant fish, but you can also dazzle them by pronouncing its native name!

Making the Fish

Cut the individual pattern pieces and attach them to the appropriate types of wood. Cut the pieces. Dry-assemble the fish to check the fit of the pieces and make necessary adjustments. When it's time to glue, cover your workbench with waxed paper to keep off drips. Glue the body pieces together and shape them as one unit. Then shape the fins and glue everything to the backing board. Apply a clear satin finish and add a hanger to the back, if desired.

Materials & Tools

Materials:
Note: All wood sizes are approximate.

• Yellow wood, such as yellowheart, ¾" (1.9cm) thick: 1½" x 2½" (3.8cm x 6.4cm)
• Light wood, such as maple, ¾" (1.9cm) thick: 4½" x 7" (11.4cm x 17.8cm)
• Orange wood, such as chakte viga, ¾" (1.9cm) thick: 2½" x 4½" (6.4cm x 11.4cm)
• Medium-dark wood, such as shedua, ¾" (1.9cm) thick: 2" x 4" (5.1cm x 10.2cm)

• White wood, such as holly, ¾" (1.9cm) thick: 3½" x 7" (8.9cm x 17.8cm)
• Dark wood, such as walnut, ¾" (1.9cm) thick: 3" x 4" (7.6cm x 10.2cm)
• Gray wood, such as spalted cypress or ambrosia maple, ¾" (1.9cm) thick: 4" x 9" (10.2cm x 22.9cm)
• Backing material, such as tempered hardboard, ⅛" (3mm) thick: 6½" x 12" (16.5cm x 30.5cm)
• Wood glue
• Waxed paper (optional)
• Spray adhesive

• Tape: blue painter's
• Finish: clear satin
• Picture hanger (optional)

Tools:
• Scroll saw blades: #5 or #7 reverse-tooth
• Drill bit: ⅛" (3mm)-dia.
• Rotary tool with bits: assorted
• Sanders: mop, disc, drum
• Clamps

The author used these products for the project. Substitute your choice of brands, tools, and materials as desired.

Picasso Triggerfish Pattern

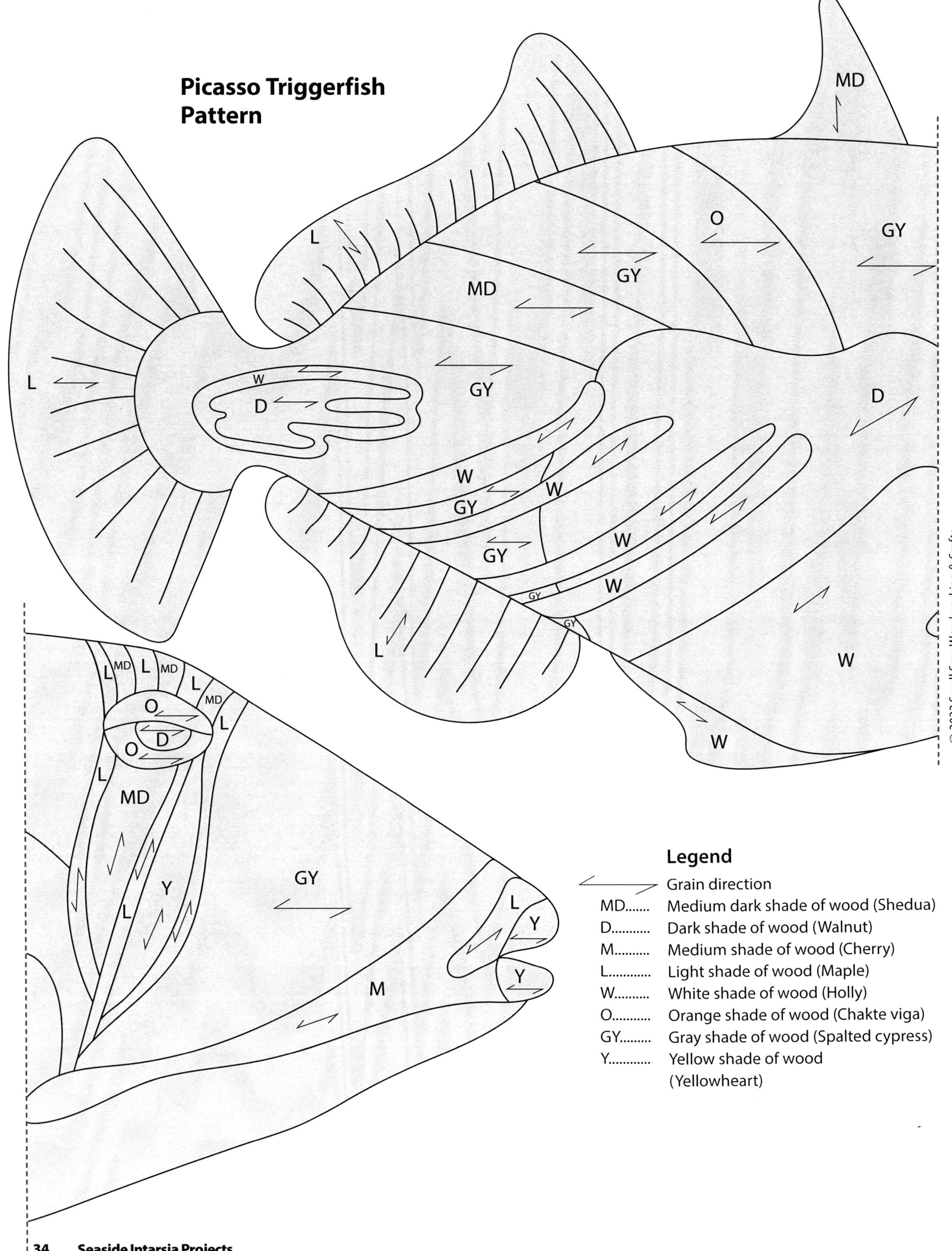

Legend

Grain direction
MD...... Medium dark shade of wood (Shedua)
D.......... Dark shade of wood (Walnut)
M.......... Medium shade of wood (Cherry)
L............ Light shade of wood (Maple)
W.......... White shade of wood (Holly)
O........... Orange shade of wood (Chakte viga)
GY........ Gray shade of wood (Spalted cypress)
Y........... Yellow shade of wood
(Yellowheart)

Sunset Serenity

Simplify this intarsia beach scene with a backing board that doubles as the sky

By Judy Gale Roberts

This relaxing beach scene is a great way to celebrate summer. The peaceful portrait serves as a snapshot of those lazy days on the shore.

Nearly all of the pieces in this project can be cut from western red cedar fence pickets. The fence pickets are usually 5½" (14cm) wide by 6" (15.2cm) long. Western red cedar comes in a variety of shades and can be found in lumber yards. The wood is commonly used for fence material and siding because it resists decay and bugs.

Make at least five copies of the pattern. When cutting the pattern into pieces, cut about ¼" (6mm) outside of the lines to provide better adhesion to the wood.

Cutting the Pieces

Cut the larger sections into pieces about the size of your hand for easier handling. Remove any tear-out or burrs on the bottom of the sections with sandpaper so the pieces sit flat on the saw table.

Use a #5 skip reverse-tooth blade to cut most of the pieces. For a better fit, switch to a #0 skip reverse-tooth blade to cut the interior lines and to separate the pieces with the same grain direction and color.

Accuracy is key. Experiment with the speed of your saw. I run my saw between 60 and 70% of the maximum speed. Align the center of the blade with the center of the line so your cut removes the line.

Stop often to remove any tear-out from the back of the pieces. Check cut pieces to make sure your blade is still square with the saw table. Plan your cuts so you can cut small parts free from a larger block.

When all of the parts have been cut, remove any tear-out from the back of the pieces. Assemble the pieces and check the fit. Do not sand the sides of the pieces. Use a new sharp blade to trim pieces if necessary. Write the number from the pattern on the back of the piece and remove the patterns.

Sanding and Shaping

I use a soft flex drum sander and two pneumatic drum sanders to shape the pieces. Remove most of the wood with an 80-grit sanding drum, and then smooth out the pieces with a 120-grit sanding drum. Finish sand with a 220-grit sanding drum.

Rough in the levels of the entire project before shaping details. Start by lowering the background and parts that would be the farthest from the viewer. Cut pieces of scrap plywood or tempered hardboard to the size of the sections to be sanded as a unit. Use light-duty double-sided carpet tape to attach the parts to the sanding shim. I use a sanding shim for the sand area, including the shadow under the chair. Some of the chair sections can be sanded as a unit to help ensure the angles match up.

Use rising shims to elevate sections of the project. Cut the shims slightly smaller than the shaded sections on the pattern. Place the rising shims in place under the pieces before you begin shaping the project.

Use sanding shims to shape pieces in sections and rising shims to add dimension to the project.

SHAPING THE WATER

1

Sand the darker water. Start with the topmost wave (33), which is farthest from the chair. Sand the piece down to ¼" (6mm) thick and place it back in position. Mark the thickness of this piece on the adjacent pieces (32 and 38). Work toward the sand, sanding each section slightly thicker. The pieces closest to the sand (51, 53, and 56) should be about ½" (1.3cm) thick.

2

Lower the wave caps. Mark the thickness of the surrounding dark water on the white wood and sand the pieces down so they are ¹⁄₁₆" (2mm) above the lines. The white wood represents the water bubbling up on the tops of the waves. Do not sand the white waves closest to the beach yet.

3 **Shape the wave caps and mark the sand.** Roll each wave cap section down along the top edge, leaving it thicker on the bottom edge. Position the last two sections of the dark wave (51 and 56) tightly against the sand and mark the thickness of the waves on the sand. The angle of the sand must match the angle on the waves so the wave appears to be washing up on the shore.

4 **Attach the beach pieces to a sanding shim.** Turn the beach and chair shadow sections upside down and remove any dust or burrs from the back. Cut double-sided tape into 1" (25mm)-wide sections, and then apply the tape to the back of the pieces. Remove the paper from the tape and attach the sanding shim. Turn the pieces right-side up and press the pieces down on the tape.

SHAPING THE BEACH & CHAIR

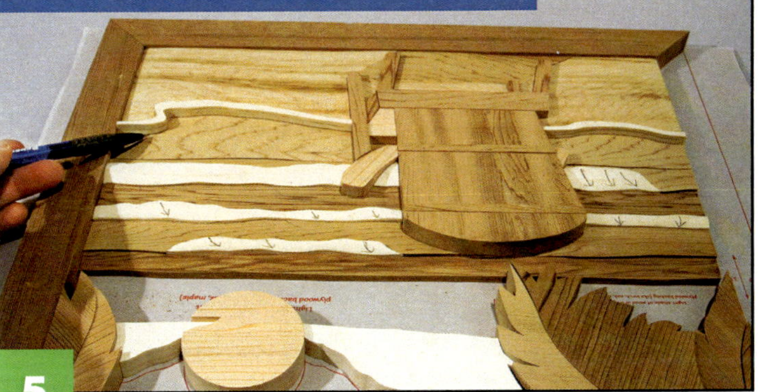

5 **Sand and shape the beach.** The beach section is thicker where it meets the frame and tapers down to meet the water's edge. Sand some dips in the beach with a soft-edge sander for a slightly textured look. Remove the pieces from the shim and place them in position. Sand the white foam of the wave washing up on shore. These pieces are thicker than the surrounding sand.

6 **Attach the chair pieces to the sanding shims.** Mark the thickness of the sand on the chair parts. The legs (60, 62, and 66) taper down 1⁄16" (2mm) where they meet the chair. Mark the thickness of the legs on the chair. Attach double-sided tape to the L-shaped chair seat and the wide sections of the chair back. Do not apply tape to the thin sections of the chair back. Attach the chair back and seat to separate sanding shims.

7 **Shape the chair.** Taper the small section of the seat (54) down toward the water. Taper the right side of the chair seat down to create the correct angle. Mark where the seat joins the chair back. Sand the chair back at an angle tapering down toward the seat of the chair. The chair back is slightly thinner than the chair seat. The horizontal parts (37 and 49) are slightly thicker than the chair back.

8 **Sand the frame.** Sand the top frame down to a thickness of ½" (1.3cm) to give the crab more dimension. Use a sanding shim to sand the top sections as flat as possible. Lightly sand the bottom frame, and then taper the sides from the thickness of the bottom frame down to meet the thickness of the top frame.

9 **Shape the clouds and sun.** I use ½" (1.3cm)-thick stock for the clouds. Shape the larger cloud and mark the thickness on the sun. Sand the sun, leaving it thicker than the large cloud. Mark the thickness of the sun on the smaller cloud and taper the smaller cloud almost down to the sun. Mark the thickness of the clouds on the palm fronds. Keep the fronds thicker than the clouds.

10 **Shape the fronds.** Mark the level of the frame on the fronds. The fronds are slightly thinner than the frame. The center ridge is thicker and the outside edges taper down. Start with parts 18 and 19. Parts 20 and 21 are thicker than the first frond. Parts 22 and 23 are thicker than the middle frond, but thinner than the frame. Keep the fronds on the right thinner than the crab and the frame.

11 **Shape the crab.** Make the back legs (14 and 9) about ⅜" (1cm) thick. Keep the other legs thicker than the frame, but taper them down to meet the body. Leave the claws (3 and 5) the full thickness. The legs on the left side taper down thinner than the body. Use double-sided tape to attach the body sections (10 and 15) together and shape them as one unit. Angle the bottom section down toward the legs. Round and shape the eyestalks and eyes.

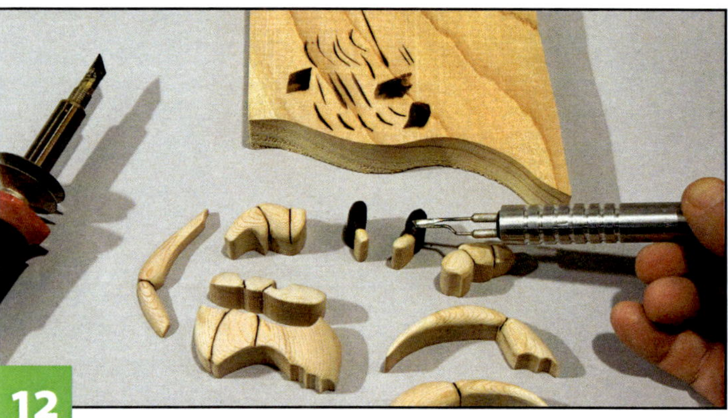

12 **Carve and burn in the details.** Sand the pieces with 220-grit sandpaper. Use a pencil to mark the detail lines on the chair, palm fronds, and crab. Add the details with a Wonder Wheel dressed to a V-point, carving tools, or a woodburner. The Wonder Wheel carves and burnishes the wood in one stroke. You can cut the eyestalk and eye from one piece of wood and use a woodburner to darken the eye, but it can be difficult to burn the wood evenly.

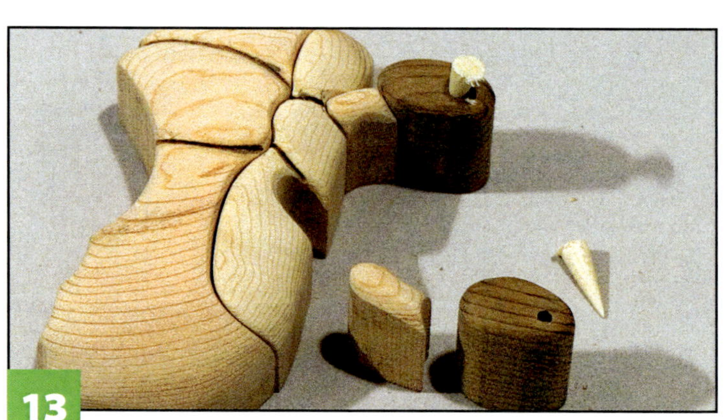

13 **Add highlights to the crab's eyes.** Sharpen the ends of a piece of aspen in a pencil sharpener. Drill ⅛" (3mm)-dia. holes in the top part of each eye. Glue the aspen in the holes. When dry, sand the aspen flush with the rest of the eye. Use a small sander and avoid the darker wood to prevent the dark wood dust from staining the aspen. If the aspen does get stained, drill out the aspen and start over.

14 **Apply the finish.** Apply polyurethane wiping gel to the top and sides of each piece with a disposable foam brush. Apply a heavy coat, allow it to dry for less than a minute, and then wipe off the excess with a paper towel. Buff the pieces completely dry with a clean paper towel and let them dry for six to eight hours. Apply a lighter coat using the same technique. When dry, rub any areas where the grain raised with fine steel wool and apply a third coat.

15 **Make the backing.** Attach the pattern to clear plywood. Cut 1⁄16" (2mm) inside the perimeter pattern lines. Use a hobby knife to cut the pattern away from the exposed sky areas. Cut 1⁄8" (3mm) on the side of the lines that will be covered by the intarsia. The remaining pattern acts as a mask. Apply clear spray acrylic finish to the sky and back of the plywood. Apply dark stain on the edges.

16 **Assemble the project.** Place the pieces in position on the backing board. Lift each piece individually, and then apply a little yellow wood glue to the back. Place the piece back in position. Use hot glue to lock a few key pieces in place. Use a level as a straight edge on the bottom of the project. Attach a mirror hanger or eyelets and wire to the back.

Materials

- Medium-dark wood, such as western red cedar, mahogany, or American beech, 3⁄4" (1.9cm) thick: 5½" x 36½" (14cm x 93cm)
- Medium wood, such as western red cedar, aromatic cedar, cherry, or red oak, 3⁄4" (1.9cm) thick: 5½" x 20" (14cm x 51cm)
- Medium-light wood, such as western red cedar, maple, or white oak, 3⁄4" (1.9cm) thick: 5½" x 9" (14cm x 23cm)
- Light wood, such as western red cedar, cypress, or white oak, 3⁄4" (1.9cm) thick: 5½" x 14" (14cm x 35.6cm)
- White wood, such as aspen, basswood, white pine, holly, or poplar, 3⁄4" (1.9cm) thick: 5½" x 12" (14cm x 30.5cm)
- Wood, such as Baltic birch oak, maple plywood, 1⁄8" to 1⁄4" (3mm to 6mm) thick: backing board, 16" x 18" (40.6cm x 45.7cm)
- Assorted scraps, such as tempered hardboard, 1⁄4" (6mm)-thick: shims, sized for patterns
- Repositionable spray adhesive or glue stick
- Glue: wood
- Tape: double-sided light-duty carpet

- Polyurethane wiping gel or finish of choice
- Sandpaper: 220-grit
- Sanding drums: 80, 120, 220-grit
- Paper towels
- 1" (25mm)-wide disposable foam brush
- Mirror hanger or hanger of choice
- Clear acrylic spray finish
- Dark stain (backing board)
- Wire (for hanging)

Tools

- Scroll saw with blades: #5 and #0 skip-reverse-tooth
- Sanders: flex drum, pneumatic drum, soft-edge
- Drill with bits: 1⁄8" (3mm)-dia.
- Pencil sharpener
- Woodburner (optional)
- Wonder Wheel (optional)
- Knife
- Saber saw or circular saw (optional for backer)

The author used these products for the project. Substitute your choice of brands, tools, and materials as desired.

Sunset Serenity
Patterns

Cut the eyes of the "LT" wood, and then burn the dark eye area. I found it easier to cut the dark eye parts separately, however the parts are harder to hold on to while sanding.

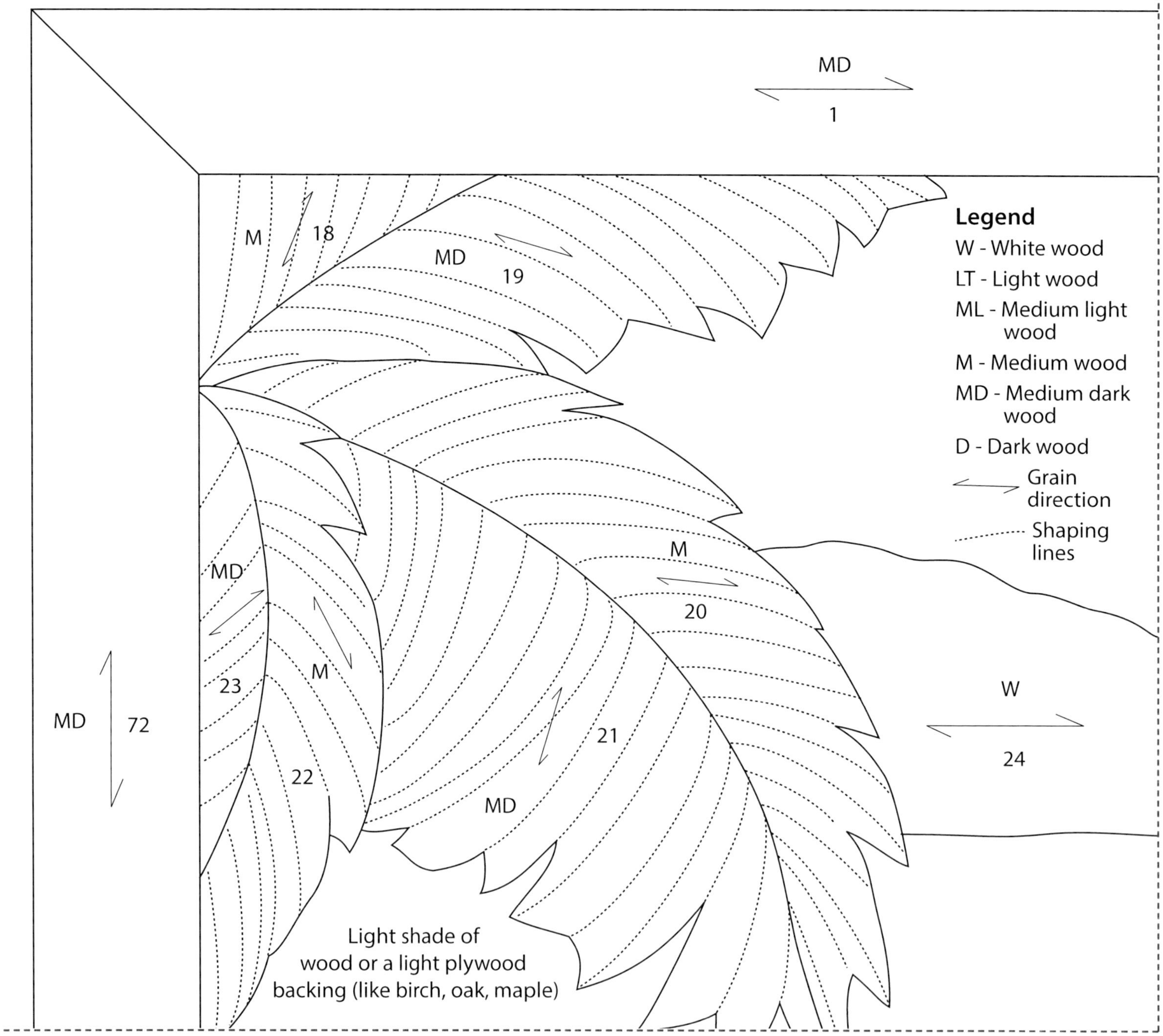

MD

1

M 18

MD 19

MD

M

23

M

MD 72

22

M 20

21

MD

W

24

Legend

W - White wood

LT - Light wood

ML - Medium light wood

M - Medium wood

MD - Medium dark wood

D - Dark wood

Grain direction

Shaping lines

Light shade of wood or a light plywood backing (like birch, oak, maple)

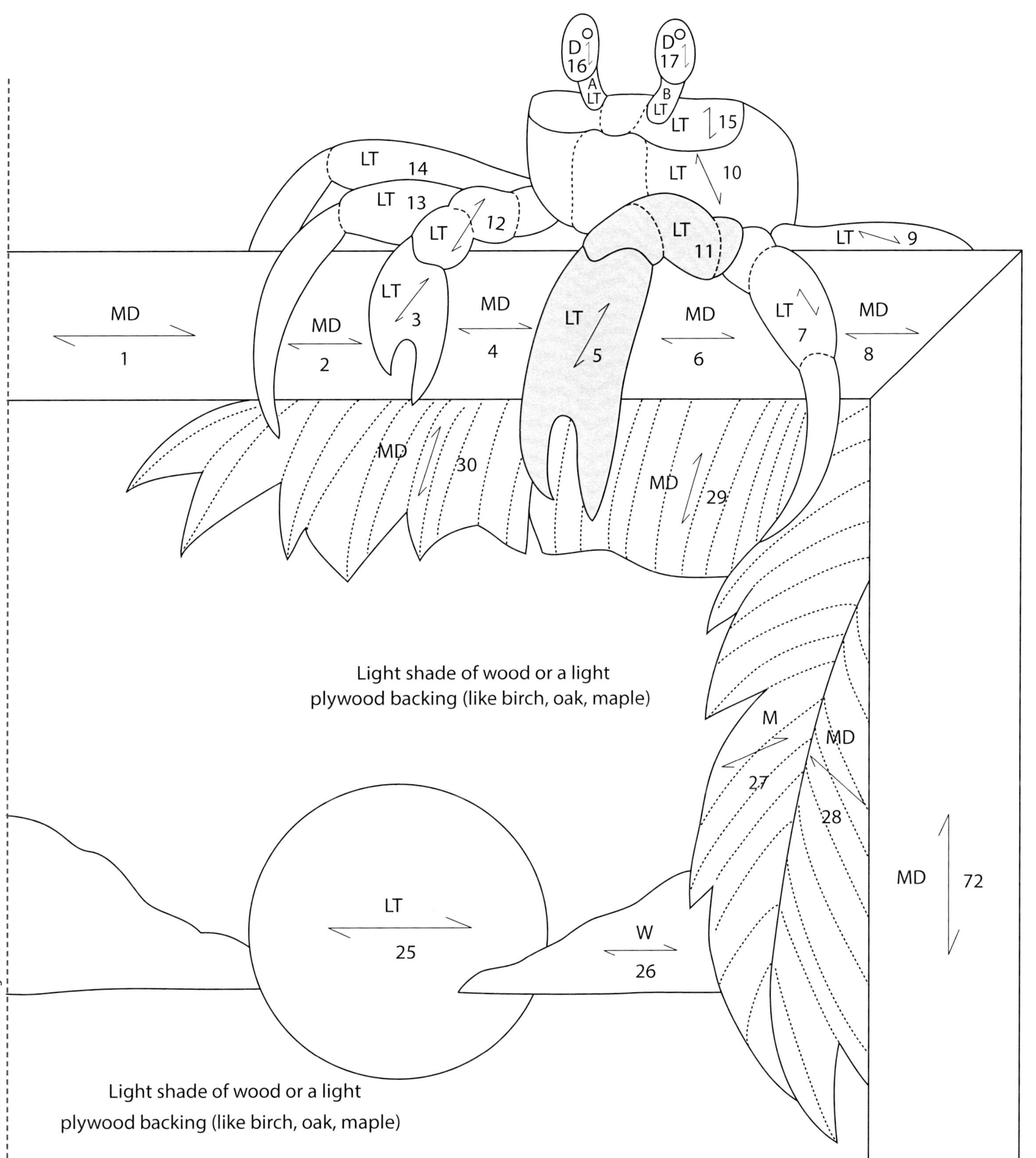

D 16
D 17
A LT
B LT
LT 15
LT 14
LT 13
LT 12
LT 10
LT 11
LT 9
MD 1
MD 2
LT 3
MD 4
LT 5
MD 6
LT 7
MD 8
LT
MD 30
MD 29
M 27
MD 28
MD 72
Light shade of wood or a light plywood backing (like birch, oak, maple)
LT 25
W 26
Light shade of wood or a light plywood backing (like birch, oak, maple)

Sunset Serenity
Patterns

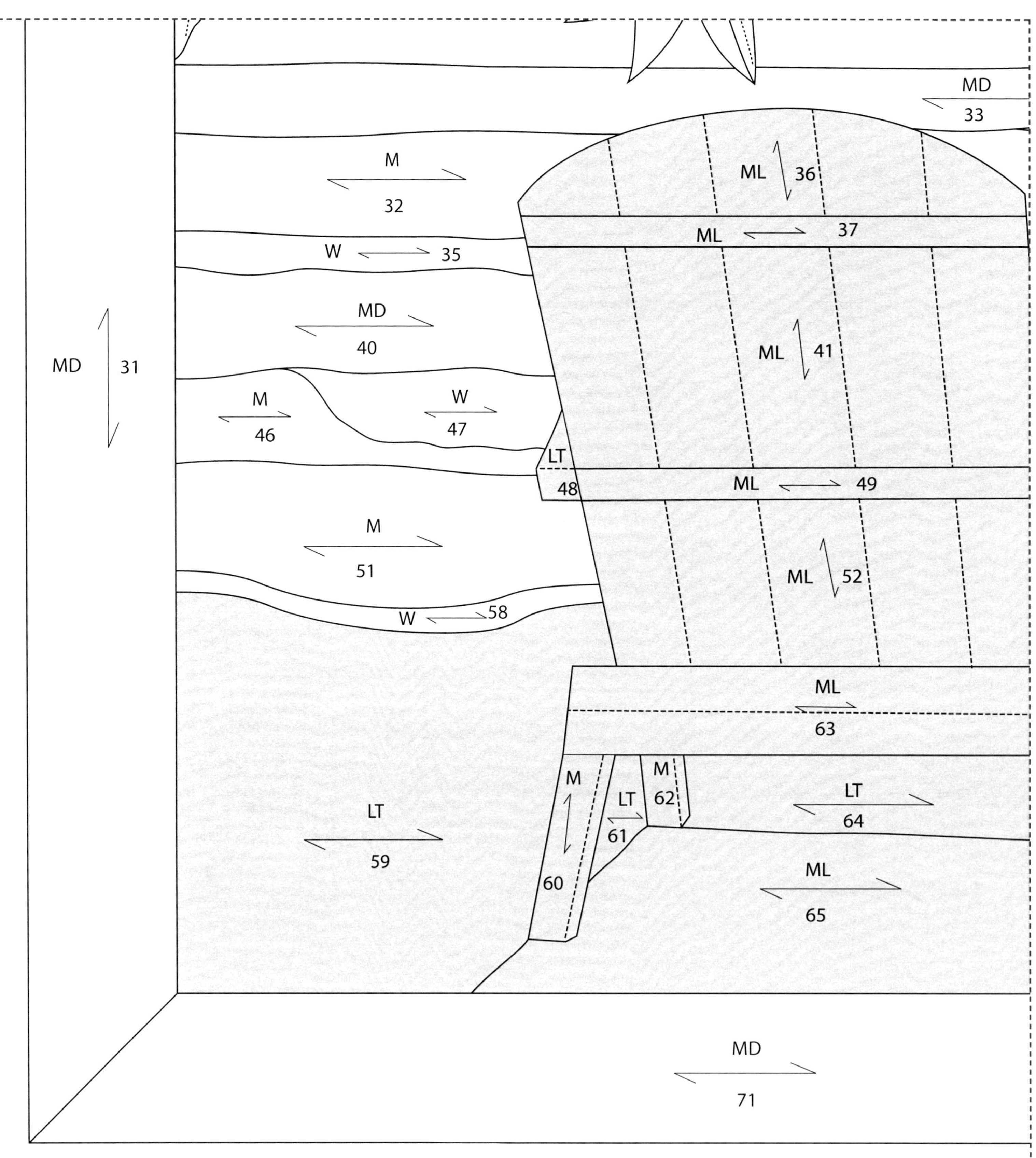

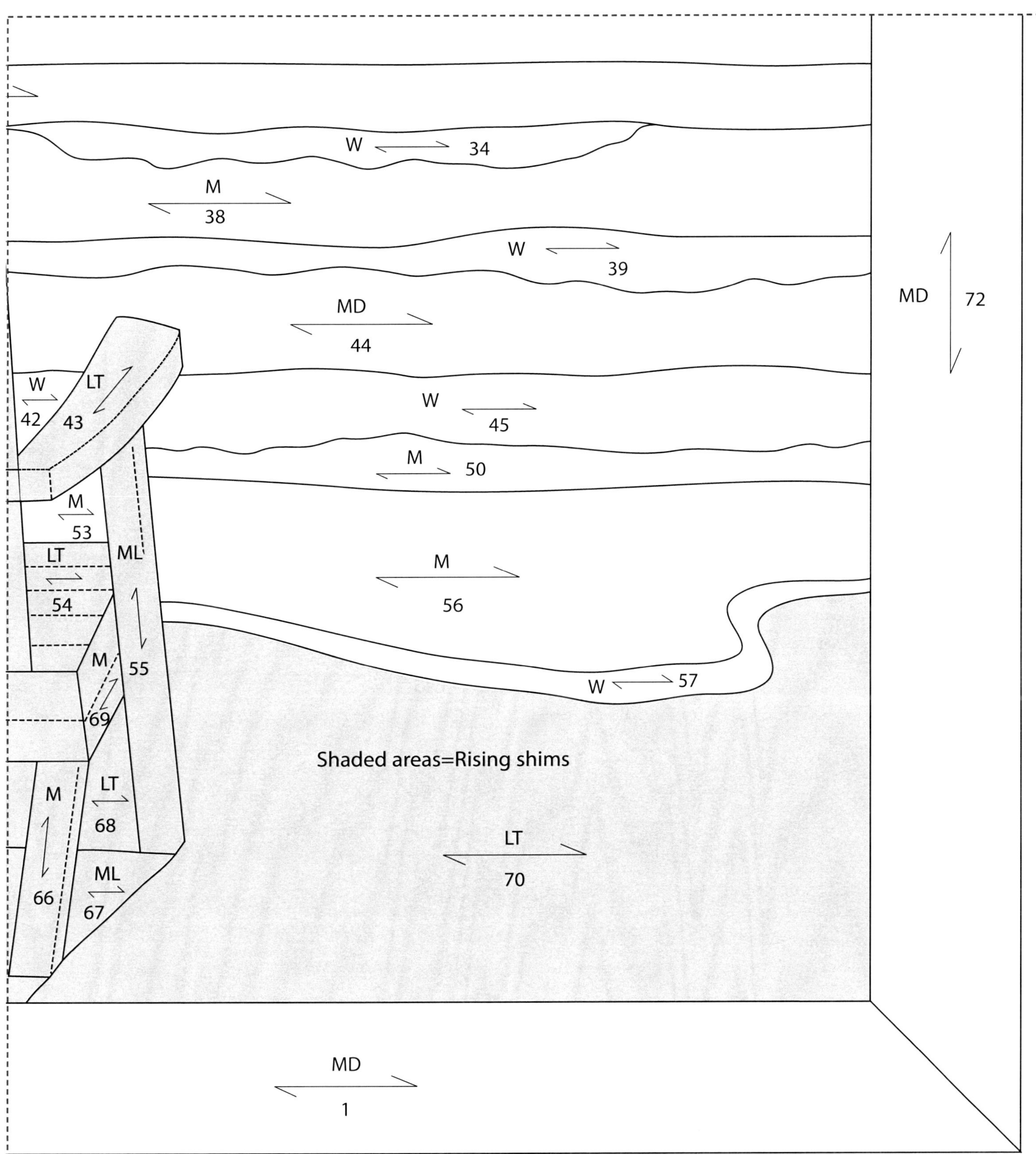
W 34
M 38
W 39
MD 44
MD 72
W 42
LT 43
W 45
M 50
M 53
LT
54
ML
M 55
69
M 56
W 57
Shaded areas=Rising shims
M 66
ML 67
LT 68
LT 70
MD 1

About the Authors

The late **Frank Droege** of Voorhees, N.J., was an award-winning, multitalented artist who specialized in painting, segmentation, and intarsia projects. His books, *Country Mosaics for Scrollers and Crafters* and *Fantasy & Medieval Mosaics for the Scroll Saw*, are both available from Fox Chapel Publishing, foxchapelpublishing.com.

Brad and Hazel Eklund have been creating scroll saw art for nearly 10 years. They have always been fascinated by the beauty and intricacies of wildlife and nature in general. Brad has a degree in horticulture, while Hazel has a degree in wildlife. They live and work next to a nature preserve in coastal North Carolina. Find more of their work at entwoodquest.etsy.com.

Anatoly Obelets of Kherson, Ukraine, has been engaged in intarsia work for over 15 years. One of his favorite subjects to portray is sunflowers; his friends jokingly call him the "Ukrainian Van Gogh." Find more of Anatoly's work at Facebook.com/anatoly.obelets.

Judy Gale Roberts, born in Houston, Texas, has long been recognized as the leading authority on intarsia. Judy was one of the first ten people to be inducted into the Woodworking Hall of Fame. For more of her work or information on classes held at her home studio in Seymour, Tenn., contact Judy at 800-316-9010, or visit intarsia.com. Judy's numerous intarsia books are available at foxchapelpublishing.com.

Janette Square currently lives in the beautiful central Oregon coast town of Yachats (Ya-HOTS). She is an internationally recognized intarsia artist and pattern designer who began using wood as an artistic medium in 1999. She specializes in custom pet portraits and has clients worldwide. Janette has been a regular contributor to *Scroll Saw Woodworking and Crafts* magazine since 2006 and enjoys teaching others about intarsia through her articles, seminars, and classes. Look for her upcoming book, which will include many skill building tips and techniques aimed to take both the beginner and seasoned intarsia artist to the next level. Visit her website at square-designs.com to see her designs, or contact her at jsquare@square-designs.com.

Patrick Wayner is a trophy husband and father to two wildling boys. He resides in Columbus, Ohio. He started working with a scroll saw seven years ago and has been hooked ever since. His goal is to bring his unique perspective to the craft. You can find more of Patrick's work at paintedpatch.com and on Instagram @paintedpatch.

Kathy Wise is a nationally acclaimed intarsia artist. She has contributed to more than 65 articles for *Scroll Saw Woodworking & Crafts* over the years, including countless articles for regular issues and additional patterns for a variety of special issues. Kathy has also written four books, and her intarsia designs are included in more than ten Fox Chapel Publishing woodworking books. For a free catalog of more than 850 patterns, contact Kathy at Kathy Wise Designs Inc., P.O. Box 60, Yale, Mich., 48097; kathywise@bignet.net; or visit wiseintarsia.com.